PROPHETIC WARRIOR

Book 5 – The Prophetic Field Guide Series

Second Edition

COLETTE TOACH

www.ami-bookshop.com

PROPHETIC WARRIOR
Book 5 – The Prophetic Field Guide Series
Second Edition

ISBN-10: 1626640084
ISBN-13: 978-1-62664-008-5

Copyright © 2016 by Apostolic Movement International, LLC
All rights reserved
5663 Balboa Ave #416,
San Diego,
California 92111,
United States of America

1st Printing November 2015
2nd Edition May 2016

Published by **Apostolic Movement International, LLC**
E-mail Address: admin@ami-bookshop.com
Web Address: www.ami-bookshop.com

All rights reserved under International Copyright Law.
Contents may not be reproduced in whole or in part in any form without the express written consent of the publisher.

Unless specified, all Scripture references taken from the New King James Version®. Copyright © 1982 by Thomas Nelson. Used by permission. All rights reserved.

Foreword

As one who has watched the complete process of this book take place from beginning to end, I am extremely excited to see this book take life.

It started with the Lord making Colette into a prophetic warrior through her time of training. He then made her live it as a trainer. Now if that was not good enough, He made Colette live every chapter again as she came to write.

That is why I know, this book, like her others will do what the Lord has destined it to do. Change lives and give His body what it needs, to change this world for the Lord.

I am excited because I know the power that this book has to change lives and be effective in the right hands... YOU- prophet of God.

There is no greater picture than that of a warrior dressed for battle, knowing his weapons, inside out at his disposal.

Yet that is still not enough!

To be a victorious warrior, you need to know your strengths and weaknesses. With this knowledge, there is no situation that can come up that can take the warrior by surprise and make them lose focus.

This book does just that!

I know that as you read this book, pieces will fall into place, giving you the complete picture.

You see, the Lord has been trying to get your attention, but at the same time, you just couldn't grasp what He was trying to tell you. In these pages lay the answers you have sought to be an effective warrior for the Lord and how to use the weapons of His warfare properly and effectively.

In these pages, you will find the authority and passion to tear down the strongholds of the enemy, and see victory as a common occurrence.

That is what we all seek, and it is what you have been crying out to the Lord for.

So the Lord has led you to this book and called you to start where it counts the most… YOU!

So embrace the challenge, endure the pressure and rejoice in the change that is to come!

Because at the end of it, you will be the prophetic warrior the Lord has called you to be and the very warrior you always wanted to be.

Much love and blessing,

Craig Toach

Co-Founder
Apostolic Movement International

Contents

Foreword 3

Contents 5

Introduction 12

    Satan has a Structure 13

    Enter: The Prophet 16

Chapter 01 – External and Internal Oppression 18

    What Oppression Feels Like 21

Chapter 02 – Satan's Kingdom – Principalities and Powers 36

    Principalities 38

    Powers 41

Chapter 03 – Satan's Kingdom – Rulers and Princes ... 48

    Rulers 49

    Wickedness in High Places - Princes 60

    Principalities, Powers, Rulers, Princes 71

Chapter 04 – Your Sword Was Made for Battle 76

    The War of the Ages 77

    Our City 78

Dispelling Misconceptions Regarding Spiritual Warfare 78

Welcome to Weapon's Training 85

Chapter 05 – Satan's Battlefield – The Mind 88

How to Overcome 97

Chapter 06 – Satan's Battlefield – Temptation Through Circumstance 108

Know Your Tests! 110

Taking It Up a Notch 113

Pick a Fight With the Devil 118

Did you Fail? 120

Chapter 07 – Satan's Battlefield – World Systems 124

The Ultimate Offensive Warfare 125

Recognizing the Attacks 127

When the Enemy Picks the Fight 129

When you Pick the Fight 132

From Infantry to Officer 138

Chapter 08 – How Satan Gains License 142

When Satan Gets Your ATM Card 143

Know Which Sin is Sin 147

Heart Sins 149

Let's Do the Three Step! 165

Chapter 09 – How Satan Gains License Through Others 172

Contamination – How You Partake of Leaven 174

Rise to the Challenge 198

Chapter 10 – Our Position in Christ 202

Understanding What Jesus Did 207

A Revolutionary Conviction 212

Establish a Favorable Battlefield 214

Blood. Name. Victory. 216

Chapter 11 – Weapons Training in Authority 224

You Need Training 225

Weapons of Warfare 226

Building Your Own Stronghold 230

Chapter 12 – Arm Yourself 244

Gird Your Loins 245

Breastplate of Righteousness 247

The Gospel of Peace 249

Shield of Faith 253

Helmet of Salvation 254

The Sword of the Spirit 256

The Average Duration of a Battle 259

Chapter 13 – Angels at Arms 264

The Omega of Spiritual Warfare 265

The Battlefield of the Mind 270

The Battlefield of Circumstances 272

The Battlefield of Systems 274

Bonus Materials – Scripture Promises 280

Healing 280

Provision 281

Victory 282

Assurance 283

General 284

About the Author 286

Recommendations by the Author 288

Prophetic Essentials 288

Prophetic Functions 289

Prophetic Anointing 289

Prophetic Boot Camp 290

Prophetic Counter Insurgence 290

Presentation of Prophecy......................................291

I'm Not Crazy - I'm a Prophet 291

A.M.I. Prophetic School..292

Contact Information 293

INTRODUCTION

Introduction

Citizenship. Every single one of us is born with it. It does not matter if you are rich or poor. You can be born fatherless and without a name, but from the time you take your first breath, you are given a place to belong in the world. You have a country or a nation that you automatically inherit.

The same holds true of when you get born again. From the moment you take your first breath as a child of God, you are born into a peculiar Kingdom. A Kingdom that has a strange set of rules that goes along the lines of, "The first will be last and the last will be first."

The King that rules us is the King above all others. Our language is that of faith, hope, and love, and our national flag is emblazoned with the blood of Christ. We have rules, structure, and One who is there to mature us to become valuable citizens, contributing to the greater good.

Is it any surprise then, that satan, copycat extraordinaire, set his kingdom up in a similar structure? Well what else did he have to go on? He was the star of the morning, having stood in the very Throne Room of God.

When you ponder the principles of spiritual warfare, you get the impression that you have demons running around all over the place doing whatever they want. However, consider this passage:

> Matthew 12:29 *Or how can one enter a strong man's house and plunder his goods, unless he first binds the strong man? And then he will plunder his house.*

This passage denotes someone who has an order - a household that has a structure. This makes perfect sense. Without a structure, how else would the enemy maintain the rampant destruction he does in the Church?

As we dive right into the subject of prophetic warfare, I want to make some bold statements to set your thinking in the right direction.

SATAN HAS A STRUCTURE

Firstly, the kingdom of darkness is just that... a kingdom. It has a set structure of government. Although evil to the core, it is well-structured and follows a pattern to ensure their morbid success. It is with this structure that the enemy imposes his ideas on our society.

He is the first to set systems in place that feed his need. When you begin to understand this simple principle, your work as a prophet will become a lot easier.

Imagine yourself as a secret assassin. You are to infiltrate and negate every work of the enemy! But, I am getting ahead of myself. Before I paint a picture of your part to play on this scenario, there are a few more things you need to know.

SATAN IS DEFEATED

Satan has a kingdom that has been conquered, but continues trying to enforce his will with a militia that uses fear to dominate those who just do not know any better.

When you understand that he was defeated and has had to hand over the rights to all the land he owned 2000 years ago, you begin to see that you are the victor. You begin to understand the fear and trembling that you bring to his camp, when you clothe yourself with the word of your testimony and the blood of the Lamb saying, "It shall be done on earth as it is done in heaven!"

And so the warfare of the prophet is not defensive. It does not come from a place of trying to convince the enemy to relinquish what he has stolen. Rather it is one of standing under the emblem of the King, demanding the rights of the crown.

SATAN IS A TERRORIST

Be that as it may, this does not prevent the enemy from sneaking in where he can to wreak havoc. With his well-placed underground network, he continues to "seduce" many to his side.

> *1 Timothy 4:1 Now the Spirit expressly says that in latter times some will depart from the faith, giving heed to deceiving spirits and doctrines of demons.*

It is when we are aware of his tactics that we can so easily thwart them! There is a strange comfort in seeing all of these pieces come together. The enemy no longer appears as a "bigger than life" enemy who has so much power to steal, kill and destroy.

KEY PRINCIPLE

> The kingdom of darkness is a kingdom that has a set, well-structured government that follows a pattern to impose satan's influence upon the earth.

Rather we come to understand that he is an impoverished king who has lost all he has, grasping desperately to try and regain lost ground.

SATAN HATES MAN

Be sure of this – satan is no friend of man. He uses man to his own advantage. Since the day that the Lord gave dominion of this earth over to Adam, satan has been trying to figure out a way to get it back!

He is known as the devourer, because his greatest desire is to destroy man, who is made in the image of God. We represent everything that he hates.

ENTER: THE PROPHET

In the chapters that follow, we are going to take a look at the structure of satan's kingdom. We will study it, as would generals, huddled together in the war room pouring over maps and routes to plan the best attack.

You will discover that as a prophet, the Lord has given you a unique position in His army. You are a spy at the highest level. You are a warrior to be feared, and a healer to pick up those wounded in war.

During the course of your prophetic ministry, you will take the land that satan has stolen. You will enter into his kingdom, on behalf of God's people, and set his systems in disarray. You will put on the whole armor of God – but not for yourself. You will do it on behalf of the body of Christ.

For just as we need a fighting force in today's natural world, so also do we need a spiritual fighting force to keep the Church safe. Are you up for the task? Well whether you are ready for it or not, it is part and parcel of your calling.

So get dressed, and get ready as we head to the front lines, and establish the Kingdom of God… together!

CHAPTER 01

EXTERNAL AND INTERNAL OPPRESSION

Chapter 01 – External and Internal Oppression

We studied the gifts of the spirit in the *Prophetic Essentials* book, and I labored long on the topic of the gift of discerning of spirits. If ever a prophet was given a gift to use in his daily ministry, it is this one!

It can be quite frustrating at times though! This was one of the first gifts that I functioned in, and at the beginning, I found it more of a pain than a use. I felt like I could feel all the demons in hell!

I could sense the conflict others were experiencing, and if there was any kind of warfare going on in the spirit, I felt as if a dark cloud was over my head. To be honest with you, I found it plain tiring. I asked the Lord to take it away.

I did not understand why I had to experience all that. I did not know why I had to feel the knot in my stomach or heaviness in the air. After I had done complaining, the Lord said to me simply, "How else could you learn of your enemy?"

You see prophet, there is a reason why you feel it when the enemy just sneezes. If you did not, how would you know he was there? If you did not feel heaviness in the spirit, how would you know when to bind it?

If you did not sense the presence of an occult demon, how would you know the level of darkness you were coming against? And so you can assume that as we continue in this book, that I will be defining that for you.

I will help you to identify exactly what you are feeling, and why you feel it. We will then move on to learning how to use this knowledge to mess up satan's plans.

You see, the Lord is not giving you visions and that sense of heaviness for nothing. You are not sensing oppression just for the sake of knowing that demons are around.

You are sensing these things so that you can know your enemy. You are meant to be using that to determine what exactly you are facing, so that you know the best tactic to use, to overcome.

For example, if I see an occult demon in the spirit, then I know I am dealing with possession, and the person I am praying with opened the door to false religion or heretical teaching.

If I am praying for healing and I see an insect in the spirit, I know that I am dealing with a spirit of infirmity. I pray accordingly.

The Lord Jesus said some strange things sometimes. There were times when he simply healed people, and other times when he bound a demon. How did He know when to heal or when a demon was responsible? Well that is what you are about to learn.

In fact, the exciting news is that the Holy Spirit has already been giving you the clues. You have just not picked up on them yet. The oppressive warfare you feel from time to time is a gift from God to you.

It does not mean that the enemy has won, but rather that the Lord is pulling back the curtain in the realm of the spirit to show you something that many people do not often see.

So bring all of that to the table. Bring the gift of discerning of spirits, and your prayer burdens and let us do some sorting.

For the rest of this chapter I am going to teach you how to determine what kind of demon you are coming up against, and what to expect.

> **KEY PRINCIPLE**
>
> The oppressive warfare you feel from time to time is a gift from God to you.

I will help draw a line between what you are already sensing in the spirit and shine a light on exactly what you should be doing with it.

So as always, I hope to bring perspective to you. Let me take you by the hand and to lead you into both knowledge and wisdom. With that being said, let's move on to...

WHAT OPPRESSION FEELS LIKE

As you studied the *Prophetic Anointing* book, I spoke a fair amount on how to sense the anointing and how the Holy Spirit moves. By now, you should be proficient in sensing the anointing and knowing when Jesus has shown up for a meeting.

With that in hand, let's take a look at what it feels like when you walk into the throne room of satan. Or should I say... when satan decides to bring his throne room to you!

Just as everyone feels the anointing differently, so also will you sense the oppression differently as well.

EXTERNAL OPPRESSION

> *Isaiah 61:3 To console those who mourn in Zion, to give them beauty for ashes, the oil of joy for mourning, the garment of praise for the spirit of heaviness; that they may be called trees of righteousness, the planting of the Lord, that He may be glorified.*

This kind of oppression is easy to spot and usually the one you felt first. When I am around a person or an object that is contaminated with evil, I feel as if ants are crawling on my head. Some people feel it like chills.

If someone is about to manifest a demon, I feel as if the entire room suddenly charges with electricity and I feel an icy chill.

I don't always recognize demons by what I feel. Sometimes instead of sensing them with my sense of feeling, I will sense them with my sense of sight.

(Remember what I taught you in *Prophetic Essentials* about how we sense the spirit through our five senses? Review Chapter 13 of that book if you cannot recall it.)

External oppression is felt just like Isaiah describes it in the passage above. It is a spirit of heaviness. You feel like satan himself is seated on your head! The very air feels thick and the light seem dim to you.

Imagine how it must have been for Isaiah – continually feeling the oppression given license to all the idol worship around him, and not knowing what to do. Well he gives a fantastic solution actually!

> **KEY PRINCIPLE**
>
> External oppression is felt most readily by a spirit of heaviness.

He said that the only way to send the spirit of heaviness packing is praise! When I feel this heaviness in the spirit, the only way to break free is through praise. Why is this? It is because you are sensing so much of what the enemy is doing, that you need a battle plan to overcome him.

Imagine that you snuck into the enemy's camp, and felt something being stirred up. You saw and felt the demons at work. Now what you need to do, is bring all of that into the war room of your Savior and to get a battle plan! No soldier in his right mind would just go running rampant onto a battlefield without a plan!

But this is what we do so often though isn't it? If you felt oppression, you either wanted to hide from it, or you waged war without asking the Lord where to attack first! You got on your hobbyhorse and bound territorial demons and demons of strife and lust. You kicked the devil in a hundred directions, and managed to give him a bruise or two. If you were really full of faith, perhaps a bloody nose.

However, was he removed from your land? Did you kick up some dust, or did you overcome? That is why praise is essential. You need to enter the throne room of God and there is no better way to do that than through praise.

> **KEY PRINCIPLE**
>
> Get into the anointing to determine how to deal with the oppression.

Do not think that binding oppression will deal with oppression. It is the anointing that breaks the yoke.

Where External Oppression Originates

This oppression comes from attack that is from without. For example, if people are praying against you, or you have a contaminated object in your home – you will feel this kind of oppression.

Imagine this kind of presence is like vapor that is sent into the air and begins to form a cloud above your head until it becomes a storm that rains down on you. It does not always start up full blown.

Some things that add to external oppression are movies that are contaminated, people that have a demonic bondage, or books that are contaminated with evil. Have you ever had guests to your home and then after they left it felt like they left a cloud behind?

They are barely out of the door and you end up in a fight with your spouse. The air feels thick around you! You might have experienced this after a movie you watched, or after bringing something new into your home.

Even Unbelievers Can Be Effected

I remember an unbeliever even sharing something with me about this (they were "godly" but did not know Christ) They shared that since they purchased one of these African idols from Africa and bringing it into their home, they just felt so depressed all of the time. They got rid of it, and so got rid of the depression.

I heard another story of an unbeliever that had purchased an old pair of jeans from a thrift store. After getting them, they started having terrible nightmares and felt constant fear. They decided to get rid of the pants, and suddenly the nightmares stopped.

CHAOTIC DREAMS

Another sign of external oppression is that your dreams will go crazy (especially if you are a dreamer). It is like you are picking up the chaos in the air about you. You dream of running or fighting people. You dream of people trying to catch you. You might even dream you are at war or being attacked.

This might even be accompanied by nightmares and attacks of fear. Your dreams are confusing, and you wake up weary. These are all just signs of an external oppression and actually quite easy to deal with!

This external oppression is brought on through the release of demons into the earth. In other words, when people sin, or speak forth words into the earth, the enemy is given license. When an idol is created for the purpose of worship, it contains something demonic.

You do not need to "believe in it" to feel it! Now I certainly do not want you to go all "prophet" on me and get paranoid, throwing everything out in your house. (Trust me… I have seen it happen!)

I am simply saying, that if you feel a cloud of heaviness suddenly coming on your head, start looking at your surroundings and ask yourself the following questions:

1. When did this oppression start?
2. Is there something new I brought into my home?
3. Was there something I watched or opened my heart to recently?

THE BEST SOLUTION

The best solution though, is like I shared already – go into praise and worship! Get into the anointing and the Lord will show you. Regardless of where that oppression is coming from, the anointing can break the yoke.

If it is someone living in your home, then you are going to be doing a lot of praise and worship until they either get delivered or leave!

If it is an object, you can either pray over it or get rid of it, like for example if it is an idol like a Buddha statue or something. There might be times when the oppression you are sensing is from prayers that others are sending your way.

When people pray their own burdens instead of the Lord's, they release a spiritual force. Remember, when we pray and speak, we release what is in our spirits. We release a spiritual force into the earth.

Now if we pray amiss, we are praying our own burden. Nonetheless, you are still releasing a force into the earth. In fact, the more spiritual authority you have, the more you are releasing. This is why it is vital, that we as prophets, guard our hearts and mouths to pray according to God's will only.

When you praise and come to the Throne Room, the Lord might show you that others have been praying against you. Now their prayers cannot harm you – but what they are doing is causing a cloud of heaviness to start accumulating over your head.

It is making it hard for you to remain calm. You feel harassed in the spirit and all of this has one purpose – to get you to stumble and open the door to sin. So before it gets to that point, get into the anointing!

Fight water with fire! Ignite a massive flame that will burn away that nasty cloud! So, next time you feel that spirit of heaviness and it feels like you are walking through mud... stop right there! Get into praise. Get into the anointing and break the yoke.

Only once that yoke is broken, can you bind the enemy and know exactly what course of action to take next.

INTERNAL OPPRESSION

Now this one took me a long time to get a handle on. I sensed this from time to time from a young age (because I flowed in the gift of discerning of spirit from childhood) but it really got loud when I became a prophetic trainer.

It felt as if the heat suddenly turned on, and I had no idea what was going on. All I felt was this awful knot in my stomach that would not go away.

So I did what anyone else in my place would do - I took antacids! That did not help. I did warfare. That did not help.

Then it suddenly occurred to me that perhaps God was calling me to prayer. And so I went to prayer and it was there I discovered that the Lord had given me a burden for someone. I was feeling their conflict in the spirit.

If you have been following me through the series, I am going to guess that you have begun to flow in this way also. It can be quite confusing at first, because it does not make sense. You will be walking along your merry way when you feel like someone kicked you in the gut!

In the beginning, I thought there was something wrong with me! It took me a few years to realize what God was showing me. Today I could not live without sensing this. I have teams all over the world and if I wake up feeling this, I know that they are under attack.

WHERE INTERNAL OPPRESSION ORIGINATES

> *1 Corinthians 5:7 Therefore purge out the old leaven, that you may be a new lump, since you truly are unleavened. For indeed Christ, our Passover, was sacrificed for us.*

> *8 Therefore let us keep the feast, not with old leaven, nor with the leaven of malice and wickedness,*
> *9 I wrote to you in my epistle not to keep company with sexually immoral people:*

There is a reason why you sense this the more you work with people. There is also a reason why the Old Testament saints did not sense it. To be able to sense the internal oppression, you need to flow in the gift of discerning of spirits.

So Isaiah knew when the enemy was at work because of the heaviness he felt, but he would not know that a person was sinning unless God told him specifically. He did not sense it from within.

When someone sins, they give the enemy license. Now you, as a prophet, work with many people and when you pour out... you open up your heart to them. You make a "spiritual connection" so to speak, and if there is any "leaven" in them, then you are going to pick it up!

That is what Paul is talking about here in 1 Corinthians 5:8. He is saying, "Hey guys, be careful! Do not allow the 'leaven' of others to effect your spirit!"

Because our spirits are now alive to the spiritual realm, it is sensitive to both good and evil, and Paul could see only too clearly how that evil leaven had a way of spreading through the camp like wildfire!

As a prophet, being able to sense this kind of oppression is a lifeline to you. When you are working with people, it is essential to sense what is going on inside of them! You will be able to sense when they get a breakthrough or not.

> **KEY PRINCIPLE**
>
> To be able to sense the internal oppression, you need to flow in the gift of discerning of spirits.

When I am ministering to someone, I often feel their struggle within. When that struggle leaves, I know that they got a breakthrough.

As a spiritual parent, when I feel this internal struggle, I know that one of my kids is under attack or allowing some "leaven" into their lives. Because we are connected spiritually, I sense what is going on with them.

Did you start a mentorship relationship and then suddenly start to sense something inside? Perhaps you felt unsettled all of a sudden. A strange anxiousness came into you – a sense of foreboding? This is the internal oppression, and the Holy Spirit is allowing it to manifest in your life so that you can pray!

It is for you to pray for the person under the attack, or perhaps to pick up the phone and ask them if they need help!

This happened to me so clearly once. Craig and I were in Switzerland and my parents were living in Mexico at the time. One evening I felt such a knot in my stomach that I could not shake. I did not know what was going on, but I just felt I needed to pick up the phone and call my parents.

It turned out that their house had been broken into and there was no one around to help them out! They were praying that the Lord would just send someone to stand in agreement with them. That was the moment I called.

I felt the attack they were under in the spirit. Sometimes the Lord will give you a vision or an impression to do something, but as a prophet, you will likely sense it like I have described.

THE BEST SOLUTION

Hopefully things are starting to drop into line for you. The best thing to do when you sense this, is to go to prayer and to ask the Lord what to pray next. Paul often said to the churches that he was with them in spirit – this is what he was talking about. To sense what was going on with those he fathered in the Gospel.

When you know who is under the attack, you can pray for them and help them to overcome their attack, or to deal with any "leaven" that they are giving the enemy license to through their sin.

If the person you are sensing this oppression from does not want to break free, you can also break spiritual links with them and put them in the Lord's hands. I will speak more on spiritual links in a later chapter.

For now, have a clear picture on the difference between the external and internal oppression.

The former is caused by the license given to the enemy through sin, objects and prayers sent your way. The latter is felt when those you have opened your heart to are under attack or have allowed leaven into their spirits (through personal sin).

This should already start giving you perspective regarding dealing with the enemy. What we call "oppression" or the "feeling of spiritual warfare" is simply the physical manifestation of the work of the enemy.

> **KEY PRINCIPLE**
>
> Just like the anointing is the manifest presence of God in our midst, so is oppression the manifest presence of satan in our midst.

So now that you know it is there... what do you do about it? Well when you feel oppression, it is a red flag to let you know that the enemy is up to his tricks. This should get your attention and bring you to praise and prayer. So without much ado, let's look a little below the surface.

Sensing oppression is like waking up in the middle of the night hearing the cry of the enemy attacking and the watchman on the wall shouting, "Alarm! The enemy is upon us!"

What you need, right now, is to know where he is coming from, what his numbers look like and the kind of soldier that is being arrayed against you.

What might seem like a surprise attack, might just be a few foot soldiers playing a trick! On the other hand, it might be an entire army, with battering rams in hand, ready to storm your castle.

So you need a flashlight in the darkness to see what your enemy looks like, before you dive headlong into binding demons and cursing satan. Well you are blessed today, because that is exactly what I am going to teach you in the next chapter!

CHAPTER 02

SATAN'S KINGDOM – PRINCIPALITIES AND POWERS

Chapter 02 – Satan's Kingdom – Principalities and Powers

"To know your enemy is to know yourself."

No quote could have said it better. It is when you understand how the enemy operates, that you come to appreciate the authority that you have been given in Christ.

There is nothing quite like looking over a battlefield, arrayed with troops as far as the eye can see, and to understand what you are facing. Then again, to see those troops be swept aside with just one breath from God helps you to understand what you have through the blood of Christ.

Now Apostle Paul – this is a general who knew his enemy, and was well versed in spiritual warfare at the highest level. There was no doubt in his mind who he was coming against, and exactly what that battlefield looked like.

He knew very well that we do not wrestle against flesh and blood! Consider this passage

> *Ephesians 6:12 For we wrestle not against flesh and blood, but against principalities, against powers, against the rulers of the darkness of this world, against spiritual wickedness in high [places]. (KJV)*

Outlined beautifully for us, this passage displays for us the ranks and structure of the enemy.

So when you see or sense something in the spirit, the Lord is trying to tell you exactly what level you are doing warfare at.

A demon is not just a demon! Just like an angel is not an angel. For example, you have the angel Michael who is the leader of the warrior angels. He leads the troops and because of that, carries more authority.

It is the same with demons. Do you see why I call the enemy a copycat? He just took what God had already put in place, and set up the competition. To be fair, it is all he knew! This helps us though to determine exactly what we are facing, and the level of faith we need to overcome.

As you continue increasing your prophetic authority, you will also see yourself being drawn into higher levels of spiritual warfare. It is why the Lord has challenged your faith so much.

It takes as much faith to bind a demon as it does to speak healing to a broken heart. It takes as much faith to dethrone satan in your life, as it does to believe a promise God has given to you.

> **KEY PRINCIPLE**
>
> What you sense in the spirit, is an indication of what kind and what level of warfare you are facing.

In fact, it just takes a mustard seed of faith to engage in spiritual warfare. You have a mustard seed don't you? Well then you are well able to deal with the pesky principality demon that lies at the lowest rank in satan's kingdom.

PRINCIPALITIES

> *Colossians 2:15 [And] having spoiled principalities and powers, he made a shew of them openly, triumphing over them in it. (KJV)*

Strong's Concordance Definition
746
arche {ar-khay'}

AV - beginning 40, principality 8, corner 2, first 2, misc. 6; 58

- beginning, origin
- the first place, principality, rule, magistracy
- of angels and demons

So these guys are the first in line. The first to be sent out - first to get shot. Some things are universal. There are scores of principality demons.

They cause mischief and cause things to be difficult for us. They are spirits of infirmity, confusion, and strife. Pesky demons that make walking out our calling a challenge. This scripture is a good picture of the kind of mess they make:

> *James 3:16 For where envy and self- seeking exist, confusion and every evil thing are there.*

In fact, they are so sneaky, that sometimes you can miss them in the chaos. You struggle with thoughts in your mind and fall into temptation. Well you can be sure that a little principality demon had a part to play in that – attacking your mind with ideas that were not of God.

An eruption of strife in your home, followed by frustration and a sense of being overwhelmed... yep you have a host of principalities having a heyday under your roof.

They serve the enemy by arranging circumstances and putting stumbling blocks in your road, with the intention to make you trip and fall. When you trip and open up to sin, that is when you give the enemy license and you can be sure that a power demon is standing by to take advantage of the opportunity.

Imagine the principality demon like a stone in your shoe. They make things uncomfortable. You do not realize something is a problem until you feel a bruise forming under your foot – causing you to stumble in your walk.

What They Look Like in the Spirit

As in all things, when we see visions, they are a type and a shadow with a message to help us understand what we are facing. I do spiritual warfare at varied levels and when the Lord wants me to see what exactly I am dealing with, He shows me demons in various forms.

What I share here might be something that you have seen as well, but it also might be different. So with each of these types I am going to share briefly how I see this demonic category in the spirit, so if you see something similar in the future, you know what you are dealing with.

I see principality demons like insects most of the time. When praying for someone, I might see something in the spirit like a scorpion or worm –both of which have negative connotations in Scripture.

What I see, gives me an indication of the level of attack, and also the kind of attack it is.

How to Spot Them

There are always telltale signs when a spirit of infirmity is at play. If someone is struggling with a sudden sickness that they cannot shake, no matter what they do, you can be sure that something demonic is involved.

You get sick with something and no amount of medication helps. You pray and it lifts for a bit, and then comes right on back! No one can seem to find the reason why you are sick! It just "is." Well I am not going into dealing with spirits of infirmity into much detail, but I am going to say this – they are just principality demons!

They are on the lowest rung of the ladder. Pawns. Foot soldiers. You have enough faith to bind a spirit of strife? Then you can also bind that spirit of infirmity!

Powers

Strong's Concordance Definition
1849
exousia {ex-oo-see'-ah}

AV - power 69, authority 29, right 2, liberty 1, jurisdiction 1,

strength 1; 103

- the power of authority (influence) and of right (privilege)

- the power of rule or government (the power of him whose will
- and commands must be submitted to by others and obeyed)
- the power of judicial decisions
- jurisdiction
- one who possesses authority

Just like their name denotes, these are a higher level of demon that keep the principalities in check. They are an officer in satan's kingdom that sends out the troops to try and get a reaction out of you!

They co-ordinate the principalities for a defined attack. Without them, principalities would just run around in a hundred directions at once, each trying to bring about their own kind of chaos. The rulers make sure that the attack has focus.

> **KEY PRINCIPLE**
>
> A power demon is the one coordinating the principalities for a focused attack.

And so when the enemy is leveling a physical attack on you, he is going to get a couple of principalities to take a hold of you. Your attack begins with a cold, then somehow transforms into a stomach virus. From there, you also suffer from an allergy... you are left wondering what is going on!

It feels as if you start with one thing, and keep hopping from one to the next. You barely get your head up, only to find another wave coming against you.

Your finances are under attack. You get a bill in the mail for a parking ticket. You pay it. You barely get over that and something breaks in your house, so you have to give that money out again. It seems that every little principality demon of theft is on your back.

Now you could spend the whole day dealing with this demon and that... or just get the guy that is coordinating it all. That would be the power demon.

What They Look Like

I see these demons in the spirit like large animals. For someone that is under bondage to a spirit of anger, I see it like an angry gorilla with its teeth bared. I might even see a viper with poison under its tongue.

When I see this, then I know what I am dealing with! Bitterness is the license given and the result is uncontrollable anger and malice.

I have seen a power demon of theft like a ravenous wolf seeking to steal, kill, or destroy. I see a power demon of divination like a python – seeking to squeeze the life out of his victim.

I see the spirit of deception as serpents as well. Fitting if you consider their nature!

The good news? Power demons know your authority in Christ probably better than you do! They know that when you stand in Christ, that they have to let go. I have had little struggle with power demons. Once they are manifest and their license is removed, they do not hang around.

How to Spot Them

They are identified by a continuous attack in a focused direction. You do not get hit with just one sickness… but one after the other! Not just one thing is stolen, but many of them!

It is this continuity that defines this kind of demon. You break one glass and you are just being clumsy! You break a glass, crash your car, twist your ankle and hit your head on the open kitchen cabinet… and you have a power demon of destruction with his crosshairs on you!

There are times when we do not take care of our bodies and allow our immune system to drop. You just feel like sleeping and taking it easy. Yes, weariness is not a sign of blessing, but sometimes it is your body's way of forcing you to rest.

You do not exercise and you put on weight. Yes, when it is out of control, the enemy could certainly be playing a part. However, if a bit of exercise brings it into balance again, it is not a demon to blame for that entire box of cookies you ate in your moment of depression!

However, if you are suffering from weight gain, hair loss, anemia, and your hormones are not coming in line no matter what you do... you have a power demon pulling the strings by setting those principalities to work in synchronous harmony.

CHAPTER 03

SATAN'S KINGDOM – RULERS AND PRINCES

Chapter 03 – Satan's Kingdom – Rulers and Princes

Now we are getting down and dirty. The first two levels of demons cause us to stub our spiritual toes and open our mouths to say things we would not. You sit in bed sick for days on end and I challenge you not to bite the head off the next person who asks you if you are feeling better yet!

"No! I am not feeling better! Now would you just leave me alone while I sit here and feel sorry for myself…"

After one financial attack after the other, it does not take much to spark of strife in your home. "What do you mean that you need more money for clothes? Can't you see I am working hard here? Can't you see what I have to deal with?"

That is their purpose. To bring you to a point of exasperation. To bring you to a point where you start seeking out solutions for your problem that do not include Christ. You pray for money and get no answers.

You pray for healing and nothing happens. So you go to the world. You start searching. Before you know it, you are looking in places you should not to meet your needs and you can be sure that a good looking ruler demon is standing by to lead you the rest of the way.

RULERS

Strong's Concordance Definition
2888

AV - ruler 1; 1

1) lord of the world, prince of this age
1a) the devil and his demons

This is how generational curses originate. Someone starts searching for spiritual answers outside of Christ. There is only one way to the Father, and it is through Christ.

There is only one way to navigate the realm of the spirit safely, and that is while wearing as a mantle, the blood of Jesus. Now what happens when you decide to take a trip into the realm of the spirit without the blood to shield you?

Well a good example of that is king Saul who decided to seek out a medium for answers instead of the Lord. He paid for that with his life. He conjured up a spirit who the witch said was Elijah. In a matter of days, he and his son were dead.

The Lord is not to be trifled with, and when you try to gain access to the realm of the spirit outside of the blood of Christ, you do so unguarded. You open yourself up to ruler demons that are ready to help you have such a spiritual experience.

> *2 Corinthians 11:14 And no wonder! For Satan himself transforms himself into an angel of light. 15 Therefore it is no great thing if his ministers also transform themselves into ministers of righteousness, whose end will be according to their works.*

The angel of light will come to tempt you, but you do not need to entertain him! If you do though, you open a door in the spirit that leaves your back open. This is where demon possession originates. It is one thing to be under attack from power demons, it is another to allow a spiritual experience outside of Christ.

> **KEY PRINCIPLE**
>
> When someone has sought spiritual solutions outside of Christ, their spirit is contaminated by a ruler demon.

That is why when someone has been involved in the occult or false religion, you can be sure that there is a ruler demon that is involved. This is also true for people who were heavy drug users.

What is the purpose of taking drugs, other than to heighten the senses and to give them a spiritual experience? This experience, having been done outside of Christ, allows a demonic spiritual influence entry into their lives.

When someone has sought spiritual solutions outside of Christ, their spirit is contaminated by a ruler demon. When they are unsaved, it takes over and we will talk about that more when I teach you about helping someone who is demonized.

For now, realize that when someone gets saved, that their spirit is renewed! That ruler demon's influence is limited, and "hangs out" on the outside of their spirits, however it still has influence enough to lead them astray. Consider Simon the sorcerer that Peter rebuked harshly in Act 8:23.

He may have been born again, but his sin and "spiritual searching" out of Christ left him bound.

BEELZEBUB

When a ruler demon is in play, you have a demonic prince that has a greater level of authority. Beelzebub is a good picture of this kind of demon, as outlined in the passage below.

> *Luke 11:19 And if I cast out demons by Beelzebub, by whom do your sons cast them out? Therefore they will be your judges.*
> *20 But if I cast out demons with the finger of God, surely the kingdom of God has come upon you.*
> *21 When a strong man, fully armed, guards his own palace, his goods are in peace:*

Sometimes such a demon can be called a "strong man" demon or a possessing demon. Different ministries have given them names, but they all fall under the same category of "Ruler." Each ruler will have a specific realm of influence.

WHAT THEY LOOK LIKE

I see these demons in the spirit with more humanlike characteristics. For example, I had a dream once of Beelzebub when I was confronted with the New Age cult (I shared about this in the *Prophetic Functions* book). I saw him as a mix between a human and insect. It was not pleasant!

I have seen the occult demon as humanoid but more like the typical picture you see of the devil in traditional artwork. I see an occult demon having a forked tongue. When I see this demon, I know that the person I am ministering to was involved in some form of false religion or spiritual act.

It does not surprise me then to find out that a past mentor was a heretic or that they once dabbled in spiritual matters outside of Christ.

I see the jezebel spirit like an old witch. When I see that in the spirit, I know what I am dealing with and how to handle it.

In the chapters that follow I will teach you about how these gain license, but there is one point I want to make clear here.

When someone has been bound by such a demon for long periods of time, you can be sure that it has helped shaped their character. It is for this reason, that dealing with ruler demons can be a challenge.

It is no longer a case of just casting out a demon. Deliverance needs to be two-fold. Firstly, you need to deal with the demon, but then you will also need to deal with the character that has been formed in the person through this influence!

How to Spot Them

This demon is most often exposed when someone manifests in the middle of a meeting! However, you will also see it through habitual, uncontrollable sin.

The spirit of death is another. This is a demon that seeks to destroy this life that God has given to us. Cancer, HIV and other diseases fall under his influences. When you see someone that continually struggles with terminal illness, you can be sure that a ruler is involved.

Uncontrollable sin and lying is another indication of this level of demon being present. We all make sinful choices, but there are those that find it that much harder. A ruler demon of lust, for example, manifests itself through addiction to pornography.

While a deep psychological need might have led the person to seek out a "deep experience" in something not of God, once that demon has a hold, they find that they "cannot" stop.

BUILDER OF STRONGHOLDS

Now there is no such thing as a victim! They can most definitely "stop" with the help of Christ! However, with someone bound by a ruler demon, it makes it very difficult. Everything in them craves to do what the demon wants them to crave.

For someone with a jezebel spirit, no matter how much they know that they need to step aside and not control, they feel pushed to take action. They even feel that it is justified!

They are indeed, the builders of the strongholds in our lives. They have built strongholds and have gained their power through choices we have made throughout our lives. I teach in *The Stain of Sin – Overcoming Curses* message that generational curses are derived from repeated, unrepeated sin. This is the ruler demon's playground.

> **KEY PRINCIPLE**
> Ruler demons are the builders of strongholds in our minds and hearts through the choices we have made.

Now like I said, just dealing with the demon is not enough in these cases. You have to rebuild the home that the demon lived in! This influence has conditioned their thinking and often the danger lies in that they think the "pushiness" is of the Lord!

Mix that with someone who is spirit-filled and you have quite a mess. Because they tapped into a spirit that was either contaminated or outside of Christ, they receive an angel of light into their lives.

Then they get spirit-filled, and the Holy Spirit begins to influence them as well. It is glorious! Did you really think that satan would say, "No problem! You want to leave my camp in favor of God's? Sure! Have a blast!?"

Hardly. He will begin with confusion and just "add" to what God tells you. Why steal the revelation when he can just contaminate it with a mixed message? Why try to stop you from running, when he can make you run harder... in the wrong direction?

This is the danger of a ruler demon and one that you will come into confrontation with more than once in yourself and in others. A straight out deception from the enemy is often easy to spot. What is difficult is when a true message from God is mixed in with the handiwork of a ruler demon!

SOLUTIONS

So what are you to do? When I faced this situation in my life, I was devastated! The Lord made it easy for me and told me to put the whole lot on the altar. My revelations, my call… everything.

He told me to even put down what I knew was from Him. I laid it on the altar and He said to me, "Now stand back… "

In the spirit I saw a ball of fire fall from heaven and consume what I had put on the altar. Once the smoke cleared I stepped forward and saw something amazing. Where my "revelations" were contaminated, they lay as ash on that altar. However, the ones that were truly of God now gleamed in the sunlight, as pure gold!

The Lord told me that day, that I never had to be afraid to put anything on the altar that I was unsure of, because when I let go and allowed the fire to come, that what was gold would only be refined that much more.

Identifying the work of satan in your life is half of the battle. When you can see him, then you can drag him into the street to get shot! The greatest enemy though is not the one that comes like a roaring lion, but the one that comes like a wolf in sheep's clothing.

The ruler demon is such a character. He is a possessing demon that has not only brought with it a skill and power to help the person in bondage, but also used that influence to shape their lives.

Never think that people just want to get rid of their demons. There is more that a ruler demon does than just lead them away from Christ.

He also gives them power. Do you think that Simon the Sorcerer was kidding when he asked to pay for the Holy Spirit? What do you think he did before being saved? He had real power!

He had the kind of power that the priests of Pharaoh had that turned their staffs into serpents! This kind of demon gives the person who invites it a sense of peace. That demon of lust brings gratification in the moment that it is entertained, with the aftertaste of guilt.

And so like a drug, the person will take it again and again! The jezebel spirit gives the person a sense of power and control. Broken relationships follow.

Beelzebub gives a person a spiritual superiority and sense of control over their lives. Temporal values? An ability to create wealth. Do not be fooled into thinking that demons just bring evil. It is the "good" that they give that lures people into their trap.

Do not lose hope though. You serve a King that has a trick or two up his sleeve! He has the power to shine a light into the darkness and to expose every true intention. He can separate the sheep from the goats, and burn off the tares, showing us the wheat.

Demon Possession: Believer vs. Unbeliever

I am going to make mention of an important point very briefly here. (I will be going into further detail in the next book in the series.) There is a distinct difference in how you deal with a demon of this category in a believer and unbeliever.

You will see so many accounts of an unbeliever being possessed with such a demon. You have the man at the tombs that Jesus set free. You have Mary Magdalene that He also set free. So it is quite a stark contrast when Simon the Sorcerer is so strongly corrected by Peter.

It is clear that Simon was demonized and even history teaches us that he started a sect that stood against the truth of the Gospel. Yet Peter did not cast the possessing demon out of him. Instead he told him to, "Repent!" This is a powerful principle!

A blood bought child of God has every authority in the name of Christ to tell any demon to flee – especially one that they gave license to. When someone is unsaved, they do not have this authority. So if an unbeliever manifests a demon, you can tell it to be silent and deal with it accordingly.

However, if a believer manifests, it is essential that you talk to the person and get them to their right mind. Once they are able to take control again, you can instruct them on how to deal with the license that they gave the enemy. They have every authority to pray, "I revoke the license that you have given to me! Satan you will loose your hold right now!"

> **KEY PRINCIPLE**
>
> A believer has every authority to tell a demon to leave and cannot be "possessed."

I have seen deliverance done like this in the lives of many believers and can truly say that it is powerful! Not only that, but because of the rest that it is done in, the person gains a greater conviction and has less of a chance of allowing that demon access again. They take responsibility for their sin. They take responsibility for taking the license away. They take responsibility to walk out their own call in fear and trembling!

So if you are faced with someone in bondage to a ruler demon, let me say this – yes you have some work ahead of you. However never get so wrapped up in the strength of the demon, that you forget the power of God.

The Holy Spirit is well able to arm you with the anointing to break that yoke and to rip the mask off the enemy to expose the ugly monster he really is. Above all, Jesus is our mighty general leading us into battle. He has never lost a war. He has never lost a soldier and He is not about to start now!

WICKEDNESS IN HIGH PLACES - PRINCES

Strong's Concordance Definition
2032
epouranios {ep-oo-ran'-ee-os}

AV - heavenly 16, celestial 2, in heaven 1, high 1; 20

1) existing in heaven
1a) things that take place in heaven
1b) the heavenly regions
1b1) heaven itself, the abode of God and angels
1b2) the lower heavens, of the stars
1c) the heavenly temple or sanctuary

> *Ephesians 2:2 In which you once walked according to the course of this world, according to the prince of the power of the air, the spirit who now works in the sons of disobedience, 3 among whom also we all once conducted ourselves in the lusts of our flesh, fulfilling the desires of the flesh and of the mind, and were by nature children of wrath, just as the others.*

The top dogs! Just like in the natural, these are the generals of darkness. These are not possessing demons – but they are too happy to arrange a meeting with one if they can!

The wickedness in high places (or princes as I like to call them) rule over a lot more than just the demons that they control. Their main purpose is to rule the systems of the world. Each is in control of a very specific realm.

That is what Paul is talking about here in Ephesians 2:2. He says that in times past we walked according to the "course of this world according to the prince of the authority of the air."

In other words, when we were still citizens of satan's kingdom, we walked under the bondage of the systems of the world – systems that are controlled by the princes of the air!

PRINCES OF SYSTEMS

They coordinate and arrange entire structures to help them fulfill their purpose.

This is where you will find your territorial spirits. You will have princes with varied influences.

To name a few of them: family generational princes, territorial princes, and princes who are in control of specific archetypes.

What separates them from the other categories, is that they build the structure in which the other demons can fulfill their purpose.

You will learn that the greatest warfare you will face will be as the systems of the world try to dominate and crush the work of the Lord. Even today, you will see ministries being crippled by financial or political attack. That is what John was talking about here:

> *1 John 2:15 Love not the world, neither the things [that are] in the world. If any man loves the world, the love of the Father is not in him. (KJV)*

Well who do you think is pulling the strings behind those systems? Now the systems in the world have been set in place by man, but the princes of the air have had a heavy hand in shaping them according to their will.

KEY PRINCIPLE

> "Princes" rule over the systems of the world. They coordinate and arrange structures in their specific realms.

So with the organized structure in place, you will find that they create the environment in this world for the other demons to perform the other tasks I have already mentioned.

For example, for a power demon to keep attacking you with financial loss, you can be sure that it is the financial system of this world that was the structure in which that demon worked!

Paul faced attacks from the political system of his day. A system that satan used time and again to cripple his ministry. Suddenly his words, "we wrestle not with flesh and blood…" is illuminated.

He realized that it was not a worldly magistrate or king that he was doing warfare against. Rather he was wrestling with the prince of that political system that had established the structure for that attack.

To overcome and to relieve that pressure, his warfare was not to be done against that king or magistrate. Rather, he had to take his warfare into the heavenly realm and dethrone that prince controlling the whole thing.

How often have you engaged in spiritual warfare, binding people? You bind your landlord for giving you a hard time. You bind your boss for being used of the devil. If you want to see real victory in your life, then you need to take your warfare a little higher than that. You need to bind the prince that is controlling the system through which that pressure is coming.

We are now starting to settle on the level of warfare that you are called to as a prophet. I have given you a picture of what satan's kingdom looks like, but it is in this realm that you start finding your inner warrior!

God has called you to do warfare at the highest level, and this moves past just dealing with a principality or two.

Your job is not just about dealing with demons in people. Your job is to go to the princes that have set things in place.

WHAT THEY LOOK LIKE

Princes are pretty boys. Lucifer himself was called the Star of the morning. The fact that I see them in this way is fitting, because of the lure that they have on mankind. They entice, seduce and invite mankind to follow after them.

When I see the prince of lust (the one in control of the pornographic system of this world) I see him as rather feminine and attractive. He is flamboyant wearing many different colored clothing. Overdone, just like the system he has instituted in the world.

When I see territorial princes they often resemble the bondage in the country. As for Lucifer, do not think that he looks like an evil warlock with horns. Keep in mind that he stood next to the Father in the Heavenly Kingdom.

> **KEY PRINCIPLE**
>
> Your job is not just about dealing with demons in people. Your job is to go to the princes that have set things in place.

A prince I saw recently was one over an Asian family generation. I was ministering to one of my disciples who was having such a struggle with generational curses. When we prayed, I saw the "prince of her family" that had been given license from generation to generation.

Not only was he the bringer of the curses in their family but was also responsible for creating the archetype and mindset that was prevalent in that family culture.

How to Spot Them

When you start looking past your daily struggles and towards the systems that are involved in bearing down on you, you easily identify the princes of air at work. Sudden external attacks that come on a church or pressure to conform to an archetype – all the workings of a prince.

For most believers, they will likely do warfare with principalities, powers and rulers.

Although every believer has the authority to bind any demon, they will not be called of God to deal with the princes of the air, unless there is a specific attack levied against them.

The rules change for you as a prophet. You will spend more time doing higher levels of warfare than ever before. It is for you to decree and intercede so that the structures of satan can be destroyed so that people can be set free!

So if the Lord has had you trying to deal with the religious system in the world so that His people can see clearly, then you are right on track. Do not try to bind the pastor that is not teaching according to what you feel is accurate. Look higher! There is a lot more here than meets the eye.

You are battling a prince of the air that has set his structure in place for some time now. There are varied levels of princes, and at the very top, you have what we call the Counsel of Wickedness that rule them all. Are you fighting laws that are restricting the church? You are not fighting the President – you are fighting the prince residing over your country.

It is time that you allow the Holy Spirit to condition you with "eyes to see" and "ears to hear" as a prophetic warrior. Lift your eyes higher! Look up and see that your place is not in casting down the rulers of this world, but the rulers of the air that keep putting people in place that they want.

Consider Persia that was as evil as it came. Yet in the middle of their rule, the Lord raised up Esther and Mordecai on behalf of His people.

Consider Daniel who did warfare and repented on behalf of Israel. He did not bind kings, but simply decreed into the earth what God wanted. This warfare did more than any weapon of natural warfare.

COUNSEL OF WICKEDNESS

As you begin to engage in this warfare, sooner or later you are going to bump into specific powers of the air that we call the Counsel of Wickedness. Later on we will go a bit more into them, but together they rule everything else.

You already know that the princes control different systems, but there are some systems outlined in scripture that we see trending throughout the Old and New Testaments.

These are systems that satan has used throughout the generations to tear down the Church, and to make sure his plan is established. I am going to deal with the three that you are going to face the most in your prophetic training.

LUCIFER

> *Matthew 4:9 And he said to Him, All these things I will give You if You will fall down and worship me.*
> *10 Then Jesus said to him, Away with you, Satan! For it is written, 'You shall worship the Lord your God, and Him only you shall serve...*

Lucifer being the king of deception, heads the religious systems of the world. Always craving the worship that was God's, he gathers those around himself that can praise his name.

When you look at the attack on Christians in so many nations, you see the work of satan. You see how he pushes his agenda in every false religion, while trying to silence the voice of Christianity.

Having done this for so many years, you would think that he would be used to the fact that each time he tries, that he gets a serious whipping. He is still smarting from the big stick that Jesus beat Him with on Calvary - a stick that we have been using since then.

Yet, I guess if there is one quality that is not pure evil that satan has… it is hope. He is deluded into hoping that he can win a war he already lost. Well leave him to his self-inflicted deception, because while he is running around with his propaganda, we are getting armed for the greatest revival this world has ever seen!

Apollyon

Abaddon {ab-ad-dohn'} = 'destruction'

1) ruin
2) destruction
3) the place of destruction
4) the name of the angel-prince of the infernal regions, the minister of death and the author of havoc on the earth

> *Revelation 9:10 They had tails like scorpions, and there were stings in their tails. Their power was to hurt men five months.*
> *11 And they had as king over them the angel of*

> *the bottomless pit, whose name in Hebrew is Abaddon, but in Greek he has the name Apollyon.*

Apollyon – one of satan's generals that takes great delight in destroying the bodies that God has given to us. He heads up the medical system of this world and when he has his way, does his utmost to keep us reminded that there is no healing in Christ – only through his own touch.

Not only is he the one who rules over all the physical attack that we face from the enemy again and again, he is the one who will keep you bound with medical bills, dependence on drugs, and chained with fear.

He warps the good that God has put in man. Man is by nature hungry to learn and keen to adventure into the unknown. God has put it in us to preserve the bodies that He has given to us. Taking this natural desire, Apollyon has used it to his own advantage.

Having battles with insurance, hospitals, medication, sickness, and fear about dying? You are facing Apollyon. Bind him, and you will start seeing the Lord work through those same systems to bring you the blessing that He intended.

I am not one that subscribes to the medical industry as being "the devil," but I will say that Apollyon has played a heavy hand in it, to control who gets what. If he can condition your mind into believing "there is no hope for recovery," then his system did its job effectively.

Pharaoh

> Ezekiel 31:17 *They also went down to hell with it, with those slain by the sword; and those who were its strong arm dwelt in its shadows among the nations.*
> *18 'To which of the trees in Eden will you then be likened in glory and greatness? Yet you shall be brought down with the trees of Eden to the depths of the earth; you shall lie in the midst of the uncircumcised, with those slain by the sword. This is Pharaoh and all his multitude,' says the Lord God*

Pharaoh, is in charge of the financial system of this world. Taxes suddenly levied against you out of the blue? How about that sudden bill that was not anticipated? He uses the financial systems of the world to try and derail the Church.

Now I am saying "try" because I have found that when I do spiritual warfare at this level, I always see results! He might try to control the systems, but I have seen the Lord pass many a blessing to His people right from under his nose!

> **KEY PRINCIPLE**
>
> The Council of Wickedness: Lucifer – the religious system, Apollyon – the medical system, Pharaoh – the financial system.

Just like his namesake in the day of Joseph, I see the Lord raising up His people into positions of power, right under Pharaoh's nose! When you realize that it is Pharaoh that continues to hold onto the purse strings of the Church, you understand where you should be aiming your poison dart.

PRINCIPALITIES, POWERS, RULERS, PRINCES

The battlefield is set in array. The principalities are biting at the bit to be let loose. The powers are focusing their attack on one person at a time. The rulers have gained their license and are building strongholds with catapults that are hammering the castle walls.

Above them all, the princes of the air pull the strings on each system, helping create a sense of overwhelming defeat on their enemy.

This is your battlefield.

And this is your weapon.

> *Philippians 2:10 that at the name of Jesus every knee should bow, of those in heaven, and of those on earth, and of those under the earth,*

As the arrows fly and a deafening cheer rises up from satan's camp, the victory shout is cut short by the violent explosion of an atom bomb in their midst. The battle has begun, and with just one shout of the name of Jesus, a thousand demons are sent flying.

Another devastating eruption is seen, taking out a few princes and no less than 10,000 foot soldiers. That is what it looks like when two of you join your hearts in prayer.

KEY PRINCIPLE

Know your enemy, but more importantly know yourself.

It is easy to get sidetracked when you look at the massive army the enemy has put into array. It is easy to forget that you have a weapon of mass destruction - an atomic bomb of power that renders their arrows, poison, and evil intent, useless. Jesus Christ, the author of our faith. He is the source of all power.

Know your enemy – but more importantly know yourself. The previous book in this series was called *Prophetic Boot Camp*, for obvious reasons. You have been trained for a purpose, and now it is time for you to begin using some of what you have learned.

You have been stripped of your own ideas. You have been armed with the grace of Christ. Now all that is left, is for you to step out as a warrior.

CHAPTER 04

YOUR SWORD WAS MADE FOR BATTLE

Chapter 04 – Your Sword Was Made for Battle

In years past, swords were passed from father to son. They were prized possessions that symbolized strength, honor, and victory. Many a sword was stained with the blood if its enemy.

Is yours stained with the blood of principalities and powers, or does it sport a neat collection of dust? Begin by recognizing that there is a war raging all around you. Open up your eyes to the realm of the spirit, and get yourself in place.

The Wiles of the Enemy

So often you get so focused on all the chinks in your armor, that you miss the huge cannon ball coming for your head!

I want you to go back to the promises that the Lord has given to you. Has He clarified your calling? If you look up in the spirit, can you say that you are still on track?

If not, what happened between God's promise and where you stand today? Now, let us not put all the blame in the enemy. He certainly has a nasty habit of speaking into our ears, but you made the choice to listen.

You did not need to be so willing to follow or believe his words of discouragement. It is time to pick up your sword. Can you see it? Is it lying around somewhere in the dust, rusting around the edges or is it sharp and gleaming in the sunlight?

The battle of worlds is raging all around you. Enter in, and let us take the land back for our God and King of kings.

THE WAR OF THE AGES

> *2 Samuel 23:10 He arose and attacked the Philistines until his hand was weary, and his hand stuck to the sword. The Lord brought about a great victory that day; and the people returned after him only to plunder.*

Since the beginning of time, there was a land to be won. The Garden of Eden was the site of the first war ever waged by man. The prize? Nothing less, than our home - the Earth.

On the one side, stood the first Son of God. On the other, was the Star of the Morning, struggling for dominance.

Satan instituted the first revolution and introduced counter insurgence warfare as he guiled Eve into sinning. From the beginning, there was always fighting, struggling, and deceit.

Fast-forward a few thousand years and it has not changed. If you pick up the Word, you will see that God has called this Church to be a city set upon a hill. Do you think the devil is just going to give us that city?

OUR CITY

> *Matthew 5:14 You are the light of the world. A city that is set on a hill cannot be hidden.*

Smash the picture of this city being built as we "whistle while we work."

No. Being a Christian means being at war. Apostle Paul did not mince his words. He said that we are waging war against powers and princes.

It is a fight. This is something that so many believers forget. If you want to learn to take the land for the kingdom of God, and you want the Church to be that shining city, you better learn to take the land in your own life first.

Satan is not sitting around saying, "If you encroach on my territory, then I will do something about it." No. He is very active in warfare, every moment of every day.

With that in mind – we have a lot of catching up to do!

DISPELLING MISCONCEPTIONS REGARDING SPIRITUAL WARFARE

It is not good enough to say, "Because I am a Christian, everything is going to go great." I do not know what kind of life you live, but that is not the life I live. It was not the life that Apostle Paul lived either. Everything is not automatically "ok" just because you are a Christian.

It is only when you know the principles, and put on the full armor of God that you will have the victory.

> **KEY PRINCIPLE**
>
> This is the truth about spiritual warfare: We want to take the land from the enemy, and he wants to take it from us.

Since the day that Adam and Eve took their first step on earth, satan was plotting to take the land back from them.

However, it did not end there, because while satan was planning to take the land from Adam and Eve... the Father was already preparing a way to get it back again! (Talk about planning two steps ahead!)

Calvary was a repeat of the battle at the Garden of Eden. Only this time, Jesus was the one with the big stick, and satan was the one having to run for his life.

That is where we stand today. We stand victoriously in the finished work of Calvary.

Do you know what the problem is? Most believers do not know this truth. They do not know that they are standing in that finished work.

You do not know it either. You forget. Satan comes, like the serpent to Eve, and he reminds you of your insecurities, mistakes, and everything that is wrong in your life. In your moment of shame, you let your hands hang in defeat. You forget the truth.

Do not be fooled - satan is looking for those open doors in your life. Some believers think that as long as they leave satan alone, he will also leave them alone.

Maybe that is good enough for the average pew warmer, but you are not the average pew warmer.

Prophet = Target

You are called to be a prophet. Therefore, you cannot sit with this attitude of, "If I leave satan alone, he will leave me alone."

Just by having that call on your life, you have been put on the front lines with a red flag and a big target with a bull's-eye right on your head saying, "Shoot me devil. Here I am."

And here you thought that being a prophet was all fun and games. Sorry about that.

Just by being called, the devil can spot you and ever since you were born, he has been trying to take you out.

> **KEY PRINCIPLE**
>
> Never forget that we are at war, and the enemy will take every chance he can to take you out.

Now that you know it, do you think that it is going to change? Do you think that by living a good life and prophesying to everyone, everything is just going to go well now? You are a warrior – no enemy in their right mind would let such a champion out of their grasp if they had the opportunity to take them out.

If you want to rise up and take the land that God has for your personal life and your ministry, it is going to involve warfare.

While you take your time in making plans, satan is planning round the clock. Now, there is good news. I am not just going to ramble on about what satan is good at.

FIND YOUR INNER WARRIOR

> *2 Samuel 23:10 He arose and attacked the Philistines until his hand was weary, and his hand stuck to the sword. The Lord brought about a great victory that day; and the people returned after him only to plunder.*

This is what a warrior looks like! Speaking of one of David's mighty men, he did not relent until the enemy had been defeated. He won the battle on behalf of others. He did the work - others partied with the fruit. Welcome to prophetic leadership.

However, until you pick up your sword to fight, there will not be any spoils for the Church.

So you cannot just work hard, put in your best effort, and make sure that you are in the spirit all the time and then think that everything is going to go well.

It is not like that. When the Lord led Joshua and Moses to take the land for the Children of Israel, they had to pick up their swords.

When the Lord gave the kingdom to David, he had to pick up his sword. Also Gideon, and even Solomon had to pick up their swords. There is always warfare involved. If you know how to pick up that sword, and use it correctly, you will overcome the enemy in your life.

YOU ARE AT WAR

You are at war. In fact, you stand at the front lines of the battle that continues to rage around you. If you were sitting at home and someone walked in your front door and began to take your favorite sofa out, would you just let them?

You would have no problem telling them to get out, or to call the police so that you can take back what is rightfully yours.

So why then are you so keen to hold onto your rights in the natural, but not in the spirit? How many times has the enemy walked into your life and helped himself to your health, finances, family... blessings?

How many times have you found yourself saying, "Well we just have had bad luck in our family"?

"Yes, it is that time of year again – the time when we all get the flu."

When was the last time you were surprised when something bad happened to you? Unfortunately, there are so many believers that live with theft, strife, and destruction that they get used to it. To be poor, is their "normal."

To suffer from fear or guilt is so normal to them, that they cannot imagine life without it. No one is taken by surprise to hear that another family member is sick or dying.

To hear that you got into a car accident or that something happened to steal all your finances, you just say, "This always happens to me." Bit by bit you come to accept these losses in your life, instead of realizing... you are at war!

It is time to pick up your sword and to stop taking these things for granted. Ask yourself this question next time something bad happens,

1. Is this a blessing from the Lord?

2. Has the Lord told me that this would happen and that it is all right?

If not, then you do not need to accept it. I believe it was Spurgeon who taught on the thoughts that the enemy puts in our minds. He said that when satan's children come knocking on your door, they have different names. Guilt, fear, condemnation and bitterness.

When you hear them knocking, you do not need to open the door. He said, "Out you stay devil! I am not adopting your children!"

In the same way, you do not need to accept the devil's children just because they come knocking at your door. You do not need to accept generational curses any longer. You do not need to open the door and let those evil orphans take up residence in your home.

You can keep the door shut and choose the blessing of God instead. So when sickness comes knocking, shut the door in its face. When poverty, destruction, theft or lack of favor come knocking... thrust those evil urchins from your life! You need not adopt satan's children.

Pick up your sword, and engage the enemy instead of charging at your spouse, boss, pastor and kids.

WELCOME TO WEAPON'S TRAINING

So... welcome to weapons training prophet. You have survived the pressures of boot camp, and have become proficient in how to "die already." You are no longer ignorant of your preconceived ideas and shortcomings.

You know that your power comes from Christ, and that your greatest weapon is the cross. You are now ready to move on to the final phases of your training. Spiritually buff and strong in the spirit, you are ready to start taking all the lessons you learned so far and to put them into practice.

If you have not already read previous book in this series, *Prophetic Boot Camp,* then I suggest that you do so now. If you take the training you gained from those principles, these are going to accelerate your journey towards office.

Whether you are called to be a son of the prophets, an Elijah or Elisha, these principles are for you. In any army, you will have those that specialize in different weapons. Some will specialize in sword fighting, and others, with the crossbow.

So your weapon will be different according to the kind of prophet you are, and where the Lord wants to use you. When my husband Craig was appointed as a prophet, the Lord gave him a bow and arrow in the spirit.

He saw that as he shot arrows into the hearts of God's people, they were transformed. Hard, stony hearts beat once again. Ever since then, the Lord has used him very powerfully working one-on-one in the ministry of inner healing. The warfare he does is close to home, and in the hearts of God's people.

So what is your weapon of choice? What has God given to you? For some it will be to engage in hand-to-hand combat. Others will be called to take to the air and "dogfight" the enemy. Yet others will be called to "mount up" and lead the troops into battle.

Regardless of your place on this battlefield, we all have one thing in common – we are taking this land for the Lord. So pick up your sword and let me teach you the "how" and the "where" of how to engage the enemy effectively.

Ready? Can you feel your heart pounding in your ears as the battle cry goes out? The battlefield is open before you and it is time to engage.

CHAPTER 05

SATAN'S BATTLEFIELD – THE MIND

Chapter 05 – Satan's Battlefield – The Mind

When you can win the war in your mind, you can win the battle. People think that prophetic warfare is only about casting out demons and pulling down princes of darkness from the air. However, when you have conquered the battle in your mind, the other battlefields are yours for the taking.

You must realize that satan has no power over you, unless it is given to him. He cannot just walk up to you one day, get in your car, and kill you.

He has to be given license. In order to get that license, he has to get into your control tower – your soul! This means that if he wants to bring "sudden death," he needs to win the battle for your mind.

Once your mind is made up, leading you the way that he wants you to go is easy enough.

So enter the principality demons. Ever ready to throw darts that will send your mind running in a hundred directions, if you are not savvy, you will fall for their tricks.

The Condition of Your Soul

The condition of your soul will determine how quickly you give in. The enemy wants to make sure that the switch turns in his favor, so that you give license to the flesh and to sin.

Once he turns the tables and you give him authority in your life, he can step in and take the warfare to a greater battlefield, and start to steal, kill, and destroy as he pleases.

This is why you need to keep your control tower pure. You must set up defenses and put a guard in place. Isn't this what Paul said right here?

> *Philippians 4:7 And the peace of God, which surpasses all understanding, will guard your hearts and minds through Christ Jesus.*

Paul is speaking about being anxious. He is speaking about when your mind, emotions and will are under attack. The solution? To allow the peace of God to guard them.

So what is the best form of defense against the attack that satan sends on our minds? The peace of God!

How Satan Attacks Your Mind

Have you noticed that when the pictures in your mind are negative, your feelings are negative as well?

From there, you start to spiral downward because when your feelings are negative, your will is going to respond negatively.

When you feel depressed, you do not feel like doing anything. When you feel fearful, you take two steps back instead of attacking with conviction.

On the other hand, when you have pictures of victory in your mind, your emotions are charged. Your will responds accordingly. You want to take the land. You want to overcome.

1. The Mind

So satan's first battlefield is waged in your very soul! He will begin by putting pictures in your mind.

Imagine little principalities throwing thoughts, like poison darts, into your mind to distract and worry you. When you dwell on those thoughts and pictures, your emotions begin to line up with your mind.

I know this battle very well. Satan uses different poisoned darts for us all, but the one that had my name on it, was a spirit of fear. Especially when it came to finances.

I guess growing up poor did not help. Add a family generational curse of poverty, and a country whose archetypal mindset was one of poverty… I had a lot to work through!

No matter how much the Lord blessed me, I always feared having lack and being hungry as I was as a little girl. The worst part is that it was so a part of me, I did not even know I was bound by it until I started rising up in ministry.

> **KEY PRINCIPLE**
>
> How the enemy attacks your mind?
> He puts negative thoughts and pictures in your mind.

The Lord would bless and before I had time to enjoy the blessing, I would remember that "nothing lasts forever." Fear would grip me and I would remember what it was like to lack. My emotions started to sway and I would panic.

MY WRESTLE WITH FEAR

No surprise... each time God provided, the blessing got gobbled up in no time leaving me in poverty once again. Then one day the Holy Spirit tapped on my shoulder and let me know, "You do not need to be bound by fear any more. You can just tell it to leave."

In that moment I realized what a huge knot I had in my stomach regarding finances. I had not seen how much fear I was in! I feared poverty. I feared not making rent. I feared not providing for my kids. I feared unexpected expenses.

That power demon was having a lot of fun with me, leading me anyway he wanted. There is a good ending to this story... I promise! Once I realized that my soul was under siege, I went into the weapons bunker and pulled out a bazooka called, "Get your dirty hands off my life satan" and sent some shots in the general direction of his head.

What do you know, the fear that had gripped me my entire life, left? The blessing that followed was a bonus, because the greatest gift was to be free of fear! To be at peace to abase and abound! The secret was found in a page in Apostle Paul's book – to not be moved by financial lack or abundance. (Philippians 4:12)

That is why the mind is the ultimate battlefield. If you can get your mind out of the way and bring the battle in your mind to a place of peace, you will be able to think clearly and get revelation clearly to deal with the warfare "out there."

How could I ever hope to help set God's people free when I was so bound myself? How could I teach, "Jesus wants to provide" when I feared lack more than I trusted Jesus?

What does your poison dart look like? What does satan use again and again to take your feet out from under you? What rattles you the most? When you can overcome that little dart and turn it around back at him, you will experience victory as you never have before.

Everyone wants to do warfare "out there" first. They want to deal with the demons in people, or the princes of the air, but what about the battle in your own mind?

Once you have a sound mind, you can pick up the faith, hope, and love in your spirit, and level any work of the enemy in the life of someone else. How can you be an effective warrior in the battlefield of God's people when you cannot even win a skirmish in your own?

So what has the Lord had His finger on? What is the one thing that He will not allow you to let go of? That is your personal battle today.

Until you confront the demons in the battlefield of your own soul, you will not win the victory over the princes of the air either. If you cannot even take down a few principalities and powers, why should the princes listen to anything you say?

Warfare takes faith! Build your faith at home. Remember how I taught you to practice the gifts of the Spirit in your prayer closet? Well did you think spiritual warfare would be any different?

You want to go out and cast out demons… but what about the ones attacking your very soul? There is no greater way to increase your faith and know who you are in Christ than to see satan running in a hundred directions when you find out exactly what that "little red button" can do on the weapon that God has given to you.

So do not despise your personal struggles today. Embrace them, because they are not just a hindrance – they are God's personalized weapons training for you.

2. Emotions

So yes, he starts with pictures in your mind. Words, thoughts and bad dreams. Each of these with a single goal in mind - to get your emotions all stirred up.

The enemy is the master manipulator, but he needs to find an "in" before he can unleash his army against you. So he will send the principalities against your city wall, looking for a weak spot.

Your wife will say something and you will think, "Yeah that is easy for you to say, you just sit at home all day and do nothing."

Your husband walks through the door grumpy, and you think, "Here we go again, he really does not care about what I want. He only cares about what makes him feel good."

You are at work concentrating on a project and you think, "I am never going to get this right. I am going to lose this promotion."

"That co-worker is looking at me strangely. They probably think that I do not deserve this job."

"The statement that my pastor just preached from the pulpit, was aimed directly at me! He does not approve of the choices I am making."

Thought after thought comes at you from without, baiting you to see where you will give in. Sooner or later something bites. Your thought turns from just "words in your mind" to a seed in your heart.

> **KEY PRINCIPLE**
>
> When a sinful thought is entertained, it begins to stir up emotions, take root in your heart and activate your will.

Eve did not sin when she was tempted to eat the fruit. Eve sinned when she took a bite out of it! She saw the picture of that juicy fruit. Her emotions were moved – she saw that it was tasty and she suddenly felt hungry.

Her emotions activated her will. When a sinful thought is entertained, it begins to take root in your heart. In that moment, the principality at play shouts out, "I found an "in" guys! I found a weak spot! This person accepted my lie!"

The power demon jumps in and says, "Perfect! Focused attack in that direction, guys. All you principalities, go for the gap!"

Before you know it, you feel angry, overwhelmed and frustrated. Jealousy rises up against your co-worker. You feel hurt and betrayed by your pastor... your emotions just got leveled by the devil!

Our emotions play a powerful part in this battle and it all starts with the attack on our minds.

The attack is the thoughts, pictures, and words that we give root. Once they are given a place in your soul, your emotions take it from there.

Before you know it, all those little thoughts have influenced your emotions, and once you feel bad, it is not easy to feel great!

3. Your Will

It is not a big jump now towards action. Your mind is filled with words and pictures. Your emotions are galloping at full pace, and it is not going to take very much for you to march up to your pastor with a "piece of your mind."

It will not take even so much as a spark to get a raging fire going between you and your spouse. Your will is fully engaged, and you cannot see anything except the conflict that is surrounding you.

What is your poison dart? Like I shared, for me it was fear. When the enemy started to win the war on this battlefield, fear would grip me so much that I could not think clearly. 2 Timothy 1:7 is so accurate! When you have a spirit of fear, you do not have a sound mind!

Facts can stare you right in the face, but you will feel defeated no matter what the facts state. Then you will act in that fear. For me, I would try to save as much money as I could. I grasped around desperately for solutions, just hoping that God would bless them. How could the Lord bless a work of my hands that was originated by a play of the enemy? How could I expect the Lord to bless a desperate act rooted in a spirit of fear?

Do you see how easily we get ourselves all bound up? Are the struggles you have with family, church, spouse, and work any different? You believe the lies, fall prey to your emotions, and then act on them. Then after you look over the mess, you ask the Lord to clean it up.

How about we go back a little and just circumvent this from starting in the first place shall we?

How to Overcome

Your first step in breaking this cycle is to take this battle out of your mind and into the open.

You cannot overcome the thoughts in your mind… with your mind! This is the biggest mistake believers make. If you are battling thoughts of lust, fear, guilt or bitterness, you cannot overcome them in your mind.

There is this crazy belief in the Church that if you open your mouth and voice your fear or the struggle inside of you, then it will come true. It is not so. That is what satan wants you to believe, because he knows that the minute you voice it, you take the control away from him and you give God license.

1. Voice Your Struggle

Voice your fears or guilt. Take them to a spouse, mentor, friend or any believer that can stand with you in agreement and take authority over the enemy.

No matter how sensitive your fear or thought is, whatever is consuming your mind, you need to express it to someone.

If there is really no one that you can talk to about it, then tell the Lord about them – out loud! Do not pray in your mind – you are trying to get what is in your mind out in the open. So if you are going to express these things to the Lord, then do so by praying out loud.

> **KEY PRINCIPLE**
>
> Your first step in breaking this cycle is to take this battle out of your mind and into the open.

Take the courage to say, "I need help. I have this strange fear at the moment." As you hear yourself expressing that fear, you will realize that it sounded worse in your head than in reality.

You will think, "What am I hearing? This is nothing that I need to fear."

The moment you put your will to action in this way, the Word will suddenly come to your mind and you will think, "The Word says that I need not be afraid. The Word says that the Lord has provided my needs." By doing this you take control away from the enemy and you expose his attack.

In that moment, you will see that your thoughts were shadows and mist that you were trying to slash at in your mind. When you stand up, open your mouth, and voice those fears, you stand up and take authority over the enemy. You take the sword from his hands and put it back in yours, and you can overcome him.

2. Renew Your Mind With Promises

> *Philippians 4:7 And the peace of God, which surpasses all understanding, will guard your hearts and minds through Christ Jesus.*
> *8 Finally, brethren, whatever things are true, whatever things are noble, whatever things are just, whatever things are pure, whatever things are lovely, whatever things are of good report, if there is any virtue and if there is anything praiseworthy—meditate on these things.*

I love this passage! Herein lies the secret to always experiencing the peace that passes all understanding!

You need to start changing what you put into your mind. The only reason he can put all these thoughts into your mind in the first place is because he is using what you have been feeding into it.

If you want to have pure thoughts that are not covered with fear, guilt and all the works of the flesh, then you need to stop feeding your mind with movies, TV, books, conversations and music that are not edifying.

You need to get good pictures into your mind. Start meditating on the Word. Start visualizing God's promises instead of what the devil keeps trying to paint. It is not just the words that you are hearing, but the pictures that stay in your mind the strongest.

> **KEY PRINCIPLE**
>
> Start changing what you put into your mind. Feed and paint pictures in your mind with the Word and God's promises.

What pictures does the devil keep painting in your mind? What is your "dart?" Fear of death? Fear of poverty? Conflict in your marriage? Sickness? Rejection? Lack of favor? Add your own dart to this list!

When the enemy paints pictures, you will see your spouse and you fighting. You will see your bank account empty. You think about funeral preparations! You imagine how much your medical bill will be…

Thoughts that have become so natural to you need to be displaced! What has God promised you? Has He promised you healing? Then dwell on that promise!

Each time satan whispers in your ear, "You feel that? You are about to have another episode..." You choose to see yourself in full health, just as God has promised!

Do not give him even an inch of your battlefield!

You can also replace the pictures into positive ones by taking specific action. Listen to some good teachings that inspire your faith. Listen to a new one every day. Fill your mind with new pictures.

As you listen, visualize what the preacher is saying. Change the pictures in your mind. Cut out the negative stuff that you read or watch, especially stuff filled with fear, failure, and depression. Get rid of it, and fill your mind with good, edifying things.

You will then find that the battle will start swinging to your side of the field.

3. Respond Correctly

> *1 Corinthians 9:26 I therefore so run, not as uncertainly; so fight I, not as one that beateth the air:*
> *27 But I keep under my body, and bring [it] into subjection: lest that by any means, when I have preached to others, I myself should be a castaway. (KJV)*

When those thoughts come to you, you can get depressed. It is very easy to do that, but do not keep falling for the same old tricks. Satan keeps putting you in the same pressure situations, and you keep responding the same way. You are like a man beating the air, like Paul describes here.

Identify your weaknesses. Make a list and realize what the main things are that you keep failing at. Realize that whenever someone does this "one" thing, you always respond in a certain way.

Recognize that there are certain words that set your emotions off in a bad direction.

Become aware of it, and instead of responding in the way that you normally do, respond with praise. Bring that body of yours into subjection!

Isn't this what any warrior of worth would do? What sets someone apart who is just a foot soldier, and someone who is in special forces? Those who qualify for special forces bring their bodies under control better than others.

They run harder, survive with less, and endure more. They do not surrender! As a prophet, you are called to one of the highest levels of office. Did you think it would be gained by a nice stroll through the park?

Want to be a warrior? Then take on the training and become equipped! Recognize your weaknesses and bring your flesh into subjection, lest you slip and become a "castaway" in the very things you proclaimed so boldly.

Think of an alternate way to respond to that circumstance. When fear or guilt comes, stop and get into the Lord's presence.

Voice your fears, speak to somebody, do whatever it takes. Get it out of your mind, so that you can get the upper hand. Once you start to overcome this battle in your mind, you are also going to start overcoming the battles out in the other fields.

> **KEY PRINCIPLE**
>
> Recognize your weaknesses and bring your flesh into subjection. Get into His presence, voice your struggles, and respond with praise!

You are going to start identifying with so many others out there that are in this bondage as well. So many people are bound with fear, guilt, and the lies of the enemy in their heads. They are too afraid to say that they sinned. They are too afraid to open their mouth and receive forgiveness.

Whether the failure is real or not, does not matter because the feelings that you have inside are very real.

Once you have dealt with the beam in your eye, then you will be able to see clearly to help your brother with the splinter in his eye. Deal with your sin, fear, problems, and conflicts first.

When is a battle won? It is won in the heat of struggle and pressure. When one warrior comes against another, the other is only overcome when he is wrestled to the ground. You will only ever know that you are free, when you wrestle the enemy in the heat of battle.

Yes, by all means, arm yourself. Get into the Word to overcome your fear. Get into the presence of the Lord to walk in love. However, it is when the thoughts are upon you, and you are in the midst of battle, that it is time to overcome.

In the middle of your conflict. In the middle of the rejection. In the middle of the pain. It is in these moments that you will wrestle the enemy and overcome him once and for all. Your weak spot would have become his undoing!

So yes, you allowed fear to force you into a wrong action. Yes, you allowed anger to force you into lashing out. Now that there is a ruckus, and all the dust is stirred up, it is time to overcome.

Get the upper hand! STOP! Stop responding to the fear in your heart. Stop responding through your anger. Rebuke the enemy until your mind clears. Calm your soul until you can begin to hear what is going on in your spirit.

4. GET INTO HIS PRESENCE

Get into His presence, voice your struggles, and respond with praise. Suddenly, your spiritual vision will clear and you will come into the presence of the Lord like you never have before.

You will experience His anointing and authority in a greater way. You will then be able to sense all the other warfare around you clearly too. However, while you have this war waging within, you cannot sense that satan has a ploy to destroy something that is close to you.

However, you do not see satan stealing ground, because you are so busy fighting this conflict in your mind. You cannot see the bigger picture. You are looking down at your shoes, and your eyes are not raised enough to see the road ahead of you.

Get this conflict out of your mind and heart, and respond with praise. Put it aside. You say, "You know what satan, I do not care if I failed or sinned, I do not care if I messed up or even if I am messing up right now. I am taking this to a higher authority. I am taking this to the King of Kings and He can deal with you."

When you do that, if there is any sin in your heart that truly needs to be dealt with, you can deal with it on the run. It takes two minutes to repent. Do not let your sin and your failures trip you up again and again.

This is the essence of prophetic warfare. When you can overcome this warfare and keep this battlefield under your control, God can use you in ways that you have only imagined.

Chapter 06

Satan's Battlefield – Temptation Through Circumstance

Chapter 06 – Satan's Battlefield – Temptation Through Circumstance

> *1 Corinthians 10:13 There hath no temptation taken you but such as is common to man: but God [is] faithful, who will not suffer you to be tempted above that ye are able; but will with the temptation also make a way to escape, that ye may be able to bear [it]. (KJV)*

I know that I need to watch my calorie intake. Then I go to a birthday party and the hostess is serving chocolate mousse. Everyone knows… I have a weakness for chocolate mousse. The diet is out of the window as I savor that chocolaty goodness, wondering at the wealth of cream stuffed into each bite. The moment is so sweet.

But that sweetness turns sour in a week when the scale scolds me with its new reading.

Temptation! We all face it at different levels every day. I chose this little illustration because it is perfect in showing how simply the enemy brings temptation across our path.

Now I am not saying that chocolate is sinful (it really only tastes that way!) I am saying that when the enemy cannot win the war on the battlefield of your mind, that he will set up circumstances to get the leverage that he was looking for.

We live in a sinful world and while you have chosen not to give the enemy a foothold in your life, you can be sure that there are many out there who are. And so he will begin bringing about pressure situations to get you to cave in.

Trust me, the enemy is not ignorant of your needs. What's yours? In the previous chapter I asked what your "dart" is? What the one attack the enemy uses that gets you every time?

In this chapter I will ask you what your "vice" is? What is your weakness? Your Achilles heel? The one thing that always trips you up at the worst possible turn? Once you know that, the circumstances that keep coming against you will make perfect sense.

Let me illustrate further.

Perhaps you are an unmarried man with the natural physical needs that every man has. The enemy will put you in situations where you will be tempted with lust. He will send a woman across your path or flash an illicit picture past your computer screen through a bad "click through."

Lust and desire rise up and you think, "The Lord tested me and I failed."

No. The Lord does not test you in that way. That was satan testing you. His tests are always designed for you to fail.

Know Your Tests!

That is one of the main differences of God's testing and satan's testing. When God tests you, He expects you to pass. When satan tests you, he expects you to fail.

> *James 1:12 Blessed is the man who endures temptation; for when he has been approved, he will receive the crown of life which the Lord has promised to those who love Him.*
> *13 Let no one say when he is tempted, "I am tempted by God"; for God cannot be tempted by evil, nor does He Himself tempt anyone.*
> *14 But each one is tempted when he is drawn away by his own desires and enticed.*

Now I am not going into an entire study of how God and satan differ in their testing because I want to move on to how you can rise up in this battlefield. For now, suffice it to say that when the Lord takes you through testing, like He did in your prophetic training – he does so, expecting you to pass!

His kind of testing is like boot camp that strengthens you. The enemy tests you quite differently. He is testing you for weakness. He does the kind of testing I explained that the principalities do to find where you will react.

Now satan knows your flaws and the weakness in your flesh. He knows what you feel guilty about and when you sinned. He knows all of your buttons. That is why you went through prophetic preparation and training -

to deal with the "buttons" that satan uses to destroy your ministry.

Of course, this does not stop him from trying. The Lord has the upper hand on this one, because this is the very thing that ends up undoing satan! When the devil tests you in an area that you put on the cross during your training, his tests only serve to confirm that you are in the resurrection phase!

> **KEY PRINCIPLE**
>
> When God tests you, He expects you to pass. When satan tests you, he expects you to fail.

So attacking your mind is a bust! What is the devil to do next? Well move on over, because the next battlefield is now in play! The enemy will begin to arrange circumstances in the hope that you will engage him and lose.

So the enemy tried attacking me with thoughts of fear regarding our finances. Well I got the upper hand on that. I rose up and started gaining that ground. In fact, I got downright angry! He left that battlefield with a bloody nose and a stinging behind to boot.

Then Entered Circumstances…

Next transition? Enter battlefield number two. Rent was due in a few days and we experienced a sudden slump. Nothing came in. Not a single book was sold, and no provision was on the horizon. I started to sweat. The enemy had mastered the torture chamber and I was feeling the squeeze.

I knew what God had told me, but in that moment, the enemy's threats seemed so much more secure. What I saw with my eyes was so much louder than the still small voice inside. This is a struggle I faced many times after overcoming the enemy in my soul. It was one thing to deal with my fear in the moment, but standing against the circumstances that were shouting at me, was so much harder.

That is when the Lord told me, "So what? So money is not in your account? What are you going to do about it? Believe the enemy or call your circumstances into line?" This passage came to life for me.

> *Matthew 6:10 Your kingdom come. Your will be done on earth as it is in heaven.*

"Hang on a minute! The Lord promised me that I would no longer suffer lack. So what is this pesky circumstance doing here, trying to tempt me into fear?"

I called that heavenly promise my reality, and commanded this earth's circumstances to come in line.

What do you know? Our 11th hour miracle then took place.

Taking It Up a Notch

So you thought all that learning you did about the gifts of the Spirit and getting revelation was for fun? Think again, they were arming you for warfare! It is only when you know God's will in heaven, that you can call that promise down onto earth.

In fact, it is a powerful weapon of warfare in the heat of battle. When the enemy tries to use circumstances to come against you, there is a simple action you can take. Pull out the promises and revelations that He has given to you.

> **KEY PRINCIPLE**
>
> A powerful weapon of warfare: standing on the promises and revelations that the Lord has given you.

Do your circumstances line up with the promises? Is what you saw in heaven clearly manifest in the earth? Well the revelation is not the problem! God is not the liar. There is only one conclusion left to make – your circumstances and the facts you see before your eyes are clearly lies from the enemy.

Welcome to warfare on a bigger battlefield. It is here that you will take ground for yourself, and those around you. As you are involved more in ministry, and work with a team, realize that this level of warfare will become like breathing for you.

The Power of the Spirit

The thing is though, if you had not taken time to hear God, you would have entered this battlefield with a stick, while the enemy has a war machine. So often, prophets in the throes of training, want to rush directly to engaging in warfare, with a weapon that is not complete yet.

Have you ever seen the effort it takes to make a sword? Those of the highest caliber take years to be made. It takes hours and hours of folding the steel to perfection. It requires the right amount of heat and cold to cure it. What kind of sword do you have right now?

Have you allowed the fires of training to harden your sword? If not, you will find that the enemy has had more practice at this than you. He knows the grade of your sword and just how hard to push it.

Did you opt out of your training half-way? If so, you better get yourself back to boot camp! You are not ready yet. Sure, the enemy might bow once or twice, but if you do not have conviction or authority, you will not be kidding anyone.

Is it no wonder that your warfare has been so ineffective up until now? How many hours have you spent in prayer? Did you forget that it is the Holy Spirit that empowers, or did you think that finding the right words would make the devil's knees knock?

You can speak in tongues or sing a children's rhyme, but if you do it in power, the enemy will be swept away with a hurricane – a hurricane empowered by the Holy Spirit. However how can you walk in that power, if you never spent enough time in His presence to get it?

Don't you understand that the greatest authority and power that you have is to be found in the Throne Room of God? Did you think that you could run onto this battlefield all alone? What were you thinking? Did you think that the power was yours?

Did you think that the ability was yours? The blood is His, and it is for us to remain under it. The revelation is His, and it is for you to walk it out. However, if you did not go to the Throne Room first to get it, what exactly are you trying to hit the enemy with here?

He just volleyed a massive set of circumstances at you, and what are you countering that attack with? A pea shooter of "principles" and "by the blood of Jesus" repeated over and over again?

> **KEY PRINCIPLE**
>
> The greatest authority and power you have is found in the Throne Room of God.

Rather, counter his attack with an array of arrows that will devastate his kingdom. There is only one way to get armed to the teeth, and it is not through more study. It is by marching into the Throne Room of the Father with boldness saying, "I am here Father, send me!"

Fill yourself with the gunpowder of the Word and aim your sights with the help of the promises that God has given to you. Then trigger that weapon with power that can only be found through the anointing of the Holy Spirit.

Paul told us to put on all of our armor. What fool goes to battle dressed for a party? Well, prophet of God, are you dressed? Are you clothed with the Word, the Spirit, and the power of God?

Before you start telling these circumstances to come into line, make sure you know what they should look like first. Yes, it means going right on back to *Prophetic Functions* and learning how to hear God.

Once you have received the direction from the General and King of this Kingdom, we are ready to take on these circumstances.

So tell me, what has God promised you? Are your circumstances in line with it? No? Well then, prophetic warrior... you have some work to do.

PACK YOUR GUNPOWDER – THE WORD

It is going to take more than a promise to get this battle won. You need a little bit of authority behind it. Two prophets can say, "In the name of Jesus, this circumstance will bow."

The circumstances will change for one prophet and not the other. Why? Nothing wrong with the promise. Nothing wrong with the revelation. The solution lies in this scripture

> *Mark 11:23 For assuredly, I say to you, whoever says to this mountain, Be removed and be cast into the sea,* **and does not doubt in his heart, but believes that those things he says will be done***, he will have whatever he says.*

Faith! Faith is what gives you the gunpowder.

KEY PRINCIPLE

Faith is the substance to the words of authority that you speak forth.

How does faith grow? I teach in my message, "Faith – the Power to Make Things Happen," that faith comes by hearing the rhema word of God.

In other words, when you have fed the Word of God into your spirit so much, it will begin talking back to you. In that moment, faith is born. Faith grows from a seed into a fruit-bearing tree.

You want to see that circumstance come in line? Do you want to dominate this battlefield? Then you should understand why I taught you how to "bulldoze" in *Prophetic Functions*. And you thought I was just teaching you another fun principle! No, I was equipping you for war!

When you fill yourself up with the Word, you increase your faith. When you increase your faith, you are a stick of dynamite waiting to take out an unsuspecting demon!

Pick a Fight With the Devil

Ok, now I do not know about you, but when I see the devil arranging circumstances to try and tempt me, I get pretty angry. When God told me that He would provide, and then the devil steals from me, well that is just like putting gasoline on my gunpowder!

When the enemy is using circumstances to tempt you into failure, he just signed his death warrant. He just put a target on his head and said, "Please, use the blood of Christ and the word of your testimony to take my legs out at the knees." I am a polite kind of person. I am only too happy to oblige.

God said He would heal you, and then your fever rose. He promised a financial breakthrough, and your promotion was given to someone else. He promised you deliverance from addiction, and the enemy tempts you with lust.

God has said that you would find favor wherever you go, and you lose an important job. These all sound like a really good reason to engage in warfare, right?

In the last chapter I dealt long and hard about the battlefield in your soul. I did so because when you can see clearly in the spirit, you are better armed to handle this battlefield.

From those moment onwards, you are starting to take the battle to the enemy. Although this battle is still provoked through these attacks in your circumstances, what you do not realize, is that you are starting to take back ground.

Up until now you have been maintaining what was already yours. To bring victory to the church though, we need to start taking more ground. Ground beyond our borders. So when the enemy comes with his temptation, be ready for it.

DID YOU FAIL?

He tempted you with lust and you succumbed. He tested you with fearful circumstances and you ran to the world for answers. He tempted you with rejection and you responded violently and let anger control you.

SO WHAT?

> Isaiah 50:2 Why, when I came, was there no man? Why, when I called, was there none to answer? Is My hand shortened at all that it cannot redeem? Or have I no power to deliver? Indeed with My rebuke I dry up the sea, I make the rivers a wilderness; their fish stink because there is no water, and die of thirst.

Is your sin so great that it nullifies the power of God? We make a bigger deal of our sin than God does. Now I am not saying that we should undo the power of grace and make a joke of it.

You will learn in later chapters exactly what I teach regarding sin. However, I am saying that if the devil tempted you and you fell for it... get back up again! Repent and pick up your sword.

You can sit and wallow about what a terrible person you are later, right now you have a battle to win. No soldier sits and travails over a paper cut in the middle of battle. What are you doing travailing over your little sin when there is a circumstance here that has the potential to steal every blessing that God ever gave you?

Get over it. Put it under the blood. If there is a trigger or sinful pattern that God needs to deal with... trust me, He will deal with it in His timing. However, let it be God who is dealing with it and not the devil that is using it to distract you from the battle at hand.

Come now warrior, pick up your sword. What circumstance is pressing down on you right now? Is it sneaking its way into your mind, gaining control over your emotions? Stop right now and raise your shield. Pick up your sword and see where the attack is really coming from.

Are you beginning to see it yet? You take your first step in warfare by defending your ground (your soul). However, the next step you take is into an offensive battlefield. One that recognizes the ploys of the enemy, and calls them into line.

Gear up, because we are not yet done. You have just begun and from tackling the circumstances around you, you are ready to march into the kingdom of the enemy and give a little payback.

Just as he thought it beneficial for himself and his hordes to attack your castle walls with fear, doubt, sickness and lack... you are armed and ready to find a few weaknesses in his defenses.

You will soon come to realize that the big show is but a shadow, and his mighty tower is built out of paper. Just as well then, we are armed with the fire of the Spirit and water of the Word.

CHAPTER 07

SATAN'S BATTLEFIELD – WORLD SYSTEMS

Chapter 07 – Satan's Battlefield – World Systems

> *John 7:7 The world cannot hate you, but it hates Me because I testify of it that its works are evil.*

There is no greater struggle than when the enemy chooses to use those closest to you to aim spears at your head. Jesus knew it well, and in this scripture He says it so beautifully. His brothers were giving him a hard time. In fact, they were mocking him and telling him to go up to Jerusalem to show everyone what a hotshot he was.

He said something that day which would take them some years to understand. He said that they are of the world but that he is not. In other words, He was saying, "You are all caught up in the systems of the world and abide by their rules. So why should they hate you? They hate me though, because I have come to expose those works that control you!"

> **KEY PRINCIPLE**
>
> The greatest attack that you will receive will be from those that do not realize what willing agents they are.

Those who have had their conscience defiled like Paul tells us in,

> *Titus 1:15 To the pure all things are pure, but to those who are defiled and unbelieving nothing is pure; but even their mind and conscience are defiled.*

We spoke about the princes of the air and how they are responsible to set up structures. This battlefield is their playground and they have been fighting here for some time though. If you feel tempted though to get discouraged, stop right there.

What might have taken them years to establish can easily be undone, and also used to your advantage! Just because satan has been put in charge of the systems of this world, does not mean we need to topple the systems. We simply need to put someone else in charge.

THE ULTIMATE OFFENSIVE WARFARE

Just wait for election time to find everyone with an opinion. They want to put this and that man in charge. However, there is just one that we need to put in charge, and He qualifies because his curriculum vitae trumps everyone else's.

That person is Jesus Christ. King of Kings. The beginning and the end... and oh yes... He also created the world. He is more than able to rule – if only He is given license to do so.

Do you really think that the right "man" in charge of your country will change everything? If so, how about you meditate on this scripture for a bit.

> *Jeremiah 27:6 And now I have given all these lands into the hand of Nebuchadnezzar the king of Babylon, My servant; and the beasts of the field I have also given him to serve him.*

An ungodly man. A pagan. An evil uncircumcised king who worshipped idols. This is the man that God calls "his servant." This is not the only reference that the Lord makes to ungodly kings. He also calls Pharaoh His servant, to do his bidding, saying that He hardened and softened his heart at will.

We get so caught up in our faith in man, that we forget the creator of humanity. The One who is able to use any system of man to his advantage. The One who can make an enemy of the crown, a turncoat, to work on our behalf!

When we give God license, He is able to use even ungodly men to our advantage. Do not believe me? The Lord used Pharaoh to save Israel (through Joseph.) He used the king of Persia to save His people through Esther.

He used the King of Tyre to build his temple! As you begin doing spiritual warfare as a prophet, I am going to remind you that your warfare is not against people – it is against wickedness in high places.

RECOGNIZING THE ATTACKS

When you realize that your warfare is not with flesh and blood, you will be armed with the power to overcome. You are battling the princes of the air who have manipulated the systems of this world to make us think and act in certain ways.

When you begin to buck against that pattern, you feel the pressure. That is what warfare feels like from the systems of the world.

When the enemy cannot take you down through inner conflicts and tempting circumstances, he will use the world around you to bear that pressure on your ministry and life.

As a prophet, you will experience this more than most. How many ministries have been disabled by the systems of the world? How many have been crushed by the financial or political systems?

So what does it look like? You just get moving forward and your credit card account is closed. You start making headway and your rent contract is revoked.

Financing is withheld, new laws come into play that hinder you, or you get audited. Can you not recognize where the real attack is coming from? Certainly there is nothing better than common sense, and if you break the law, then you are certainly opening up yourself for attack.

However, there are times when the attack comes out of nowhere and you can feel the enemy all over it. Now learning how to use the systems to your advantage is a message for another place. Now, I want to focus on how to deal with this kind of warfare and when to deal with it.

Offensive Warfare

So when is the right time to engage in this kind of warfare? Well there are two specific times. There are times when the devil picks a fight with you and then… well… he just asked for it then, didn't he?

Then there are other times when the Lord will bring it up during your times of intercession. You will be called to take back the land that the enemy has stolen from you, or from God's people.

The time not to enter into this warfare is when your views are colored by pre-conceived ideas! Got a bone to pick with the medical system? Now is not the time to wage a war unarmed and unled! Never forget, that you never enter into warfare alone. The Holy Spirit is your warrior-at-arms who will keep you armored and anointed.

If you decided to go unled into such warfare, you will be like a lone little foot soldier standing in the middle of the battlefield with a big red flag shouting, "Here I am guys! Come and get me!" If you step onto that battlefield without the Holy Spirit, do not be all crushed when He is not there to follow up your fleshly ambitions.

Yes, it is true that the enemy has to bow at the name of Jesus. If you really want to march into the enemies' camp just for the fun of it, to beat him up, you can do that. Like I said before, you might even give him a bloody nose and so feel good about yourself. However, what kind of change came about from your time of warfare?

Was a system changed? Was the Lord Jesus put on the throne? Did you see results, or did you just feel good about yourself because you have a bit of authority to throw around?

Never forget, spiritual warfare should always have purpose. If you want to hit the enemy quick and hard, you need to have a plan and focus. You can only get either of these from being in communication with the Father. So yes... back to the Throne Room for you!

WHEN THE ENEMY PICKS THE FIGHT

So the enemy is the one that started it! You were serving the Lord and taking ground, when he decided to sneak into your camp with an attack from one of the systems of the world. He just picked a fight and it is time to take back that land.

> **KEY PRINCIPLE**
> Always remember that Holy Spirit is your warrior-at-arms who will keep you armored and anointed.

He should have known better! That is why it is vital to have your daily "stand to" like I taught you in the *Prophetic Anointing* book. Be aware of when the enemy is sneaking in with his surprise attacks.

The most important part is to identify the attack! As strange as it might sound to you, there are many who are being hammered with a shower of boulders being aimed at their castle, and they do not see it.

They hear the thundering hammer of another rock hitting their roof and they say, "Yep, it's raining again. Same as it always is." They are so used to wave after wave of attacks that the next time they experience loss and theft, they just take it lying down.

So engaging in this spiritual warfare begins with identifying it! (I will go into this more in the next chapter).

> *Deuteronomy 28:7 The Lord will cause your enemies who rise against you to be defeated before your face; they shall come out against you one way and flee before you seven ways.*

When the enemy comes against you, now is the time to attack. It is time to take authority over this oppression. The best kind of warfare is not just binding demons though. The best kind of attack is so much more powerful than that.

Why fight demons, when you can just give their throne to Jesus? See what I am saying here? How long do you spend binding demons and how much time do you take to give Jesus the authority to send the enemy running in seven directions?

You want to cripple satan's works in this world? Then give God license. So yes, by all means bind the enemy. Tell him to get his hands off your health, finances and ministry. That is the quick part.

Where you should be taking your time to pray things through is in giving God control of that system. Give the Holy Spirit license to use that system to His own end. Look at your circumstances. Look at the promises God has made and call those systems into line according to God's plan!

When the systems fall into line with the plan that God has instituted in this world, the blessing is natural. When Jesus is at the helm, you can be sure that He is swaying things in your favor.

So yes, run around and dethrone the devil. Who are you putting back in his place? There is no shortage of demons out there. I am sure that the next guy is just ready to jump on in. Your spiritual warfare is not done until Jesus has been crowned and given His correct place on the throne of the systems of the world. Powerful isn't it? Your times of spiritual warfare are about to explode!

WHEN YOU PICK THE FIGHT

Now we are getting down and dirty! You have learned to overcome the enemy in your life. Up until now the Lord has been stretching you. You have been dealing with the open doors in your life. You have been building up your faith!

With each conflict you overcame in your mind, you took back a bit more ground. Every single time you recognized a temptation, and stood against it with a new conviction, your faith grew!

There is a reason why you have faced the storms that you have. They have been buffeting that flesh of yours. They have been training you like a gladiator of old. And just like in the times of gladiators, this is a fight to the death.

This is a fight on behalf of God's people to take them back from the clutches of the enemy. This is no game. If you mess up in personal warfare, you are the one that suffers. When you mess up on the battlefield of the systems, it is the Church that pays the price.

So take your time in learning how to overcome the enemy in your personal life. In fact, it might have felt to you that since beginning this book, the things that you have struggled with from the past, have resurfaced and increased.

Increased physical attack. Increased financial attack. Increased conflicts and opposition. Good! Each of these are making your arms strong. Tell me, how did Samson handle this kind of attack?

He was led away by the Philistines, all tied up. Did he say to himself, "God called me to be a deliverer, but my people gave me up to the enemy! My attack came from those closest to me. I am going to give up!"

Not Samson. He thought to himself, "Here I am, being led by the Philistines, all tied up. Perfect! What can I get my hands on?"

The Philistines did not know what hit them. Perhaps a few got a quick glimpse of that donkey bone just before their lights went out.

Samson did not consider the attacks of the system as an opportunity to give up. He saw it as an opportunity to give the enemy a whipping he would never forget!

It got even worse for him after that. Fair enough... he made one or two bad choices. Those choices resulted in him being tied to a few pillars in a pagan temple. He was bound and blind. Still a reason to complain? Samson saw it as the opportunity of a lifetime. For all his fleshly weaknesses, you have to love the purity of this man's unconquerable spirit!

He took down more on the day of his death, than while he lived. He never saw the attack of the enemy as an opportunity to give up. He saw it as an epic opportunity to take them out from right within their own camp.

So has the enemy dragged you into his camp? Oh boy, do you have an opportunity! He just showed you his hand. Time to get to action, prophetic warrior. Time to put aside your sin, failure and what you feel. It is time for you to say, "Now where did I leave that donkey jawbone lying around…"

Each bout with the enemy has strengthened your arms. Each battlefield that you have faced, has educated you on the tactics of the enemy. So do not give up now, because you are about to experience the good part!

Taking Land for Others

There is no better time to pick a fight with the devil than when the Lord tells you to. Again and again, the Lord told Joshua to be strong and to claim the land that his foot touched. After some time of planning and walking around, it was time to raise his sword.

As you enter into intercession and ask the Lord to use you, he will begin to give you burdens of warfare. He will draw you onto this battlefield and lay open His plans to you.

I remember a time when I was quite active in spiritual warfare. Out of the blue the Lord changed tactics on me. He said, "Ok Colette, no more warfare."

"Huh? Is that you Lord? You sure that I heard that right?"

"You heard me. No more spiritual warfare. Ignore the devil for now."

I thought I was losing it. I listened to the Lord (skeptically) and continued to follow His lead. What I did not anticipate was that He was leading me into a season of being equipped and fitted for a new set of armor.

He led me into the Word, and my teacher training commenced. Any "warfare" I did, for a long time was simply standing on the Word and declaring it so. He taught me to close all open doors to the enemy. He was teaching me another way to fight.

Just like a good soldier is equipped with many fighting styles, the Lord was training me in an area I had not known up until then. I learned how powerful faith was. That it was a greater weapon than binding any demon!

When I had faith in the Lord, the demons trembled automatically. When I walked in love, satan could not touch me! When I focused on hope, the enemy could not distract me with circumstances.

Instead of doing spiritual warfare by binding demons, I did so by living the crucified life of Christ. It was one of the most revolutionary trainings I had ever experienced. I loved it. I had never felt so equipped. Always a prophet at heart though, this became my new "thing" and a hobby horse.

Why do spiritual warfare when you can just walk in the spirit?

Well that is when the Lord said to me, "Colette you know how I said no spiritual warfare?"

"Yes Lord."

"Great, ignore that. It is time to do warfare daily now."

"What?"

I was ready, and when I entered the battlefield again, I discovered a newfound authority. You see, I had learned to maintain my ground through the Word and the Spirit.

By using faith alone to overcome the enemy, I had built some pretty big spiritual muscles. I am sharing this, because I want you to know that no matter how strong you think the devil is, faith in Jesus is the greatest weapon of all.

By not doing spiritual warfare and just "faith-ing it," my spiritual muscles became strong. I was continually wrestling against an enemy that was just a bit stronger than me. Then one day my faith swung the balance, and I won the fight.

> **KEY PRINCIPLE**
>
> When you have faith in the Lord, walk in love, and focus on hope, satan cannot touch you or distract you with circumstances.

Without having to bind a single demon, my faith outmatched the attack around me. I had pushed the devil back. Once I had become strong in my spirit, the Lord now said it was time to engage in more active warfare.

He was leading us, as a ministry, to move out more internationally, and the work needed to grow fast. So it was time to clear the ground so that we could start building. You see, the enemy makes it that much harder to get things done in this world.

He puts up stumbling blocks. He discourages us. He brings fear and strife to slow you down. He causes circumstances to steal finances, and systems of the world to hinder you. By the use of pure faith alone, you can overcome! By walking in the spirit alone, you can win the battle.

The blood of Jesus is stronger than any attack. The thing is, without engaging in spiritual warfare, it will just take longer. You will have to "wrestle through" the fear with the Word. You will have to stand on the Word again and again until your faith has grown to the point where your spiritual armor is like crocodile skin!

Now there is an easier way! You can bind the spirit of fear and then use your faith to build the new plan that God has drawn up. The Lord made me do both, and I highly recommend it to any prophetic warrior.

By binding the devil, I leveled the battlefield, which meant that I could immediately begin giving the Lord license over those systems. However, when the Lord held me back to strengthen my faith, when I returned to the battlefield, I did not do so as the little foot soldier that I had started out as.

From Infantry to Officer

When I first discovered the battlefields of the enemy, I was young and was feeling my way around. The more I learned about my authority, the more damage I could do. Still, my weapons were more like slings and stones with an arrow or two.

> **Key Principle**
>
> Know your enemy. Know his battlefield, but more importantly know yourself. Know what it is that God has put you in this earth for.

Returning to the battlefield after intense training in the Word, was a different story altogether. I was no longer little David standing up against Goliath. The tables had turned. I was the Goliath now and the enemy was cowering before me.

I stood up as the warrior that God had wrought in me and I did so without fear. I did not doubt that the enemy should bow. I did not fear the consequences. It no longer occurred to me that the enemy would not bow.

It did not take me an hour of warfare to clear the battlefield. It took just one word. Now I was ready. I was finally a prophetic warrior.

This is what the Holy Spirit is forming in you right now. Not just someone that can throw around a few sticks and stones. He would rather you raised a sword of immense power and authority.

So know your enemy. Know his battlefield, but more importantly know yourself. Know what it is that God has put you in this earth for. You are not called to wage war just for yourself.

You are called as an officer of the Most High God. You are called to uphold His laws and to ensure that the throne of Christ remains secure. This is the core of spiritual warfare and your place as a prophetic warrior.

CHAPTER 08

HOW SATAN GAINS LICENSE

Chapter 08 – How Satan Gains License

So why all this effort? Why doesn't the enemy just wipe you out? Why this elaborate plan to try to trip you up? It is because the enemy knows a bit more about his rights than you do. Let me illustrate.

We do a lot of traveling in my family, so we rely heavily on online banking to know what our balances are.

One Saturday morning I logged into one of our bank accounts and saw that $500 had been withdrawn. I could not call the bank to find out what was going on because it was over the weekend and they were closed that day. So, I had to wait.

I checked again on Sunday - another $500 had been withdrawn. I was still unable to do anything because it was still over the weekend. Then, on Monday, another $500 was deducted from our account again.

I nearly had a heart attack on the spot. I could not believe it. I finally got in touch with the bank early Monday morning and I could not believe what I heard. I do not know how, but someone made a copy of our ATM card and even found out the PIN code.

So, the thieves were able to go to an ATM machine and draw the money straight out. I was flabbergasted. Thank the Lord that the bank we were with was able to refund the money to us because it was covered under the insurance.

In the end, the Lord protected us, but it was still a horrible experience. You are walking along and suddenly the enemy just jumps in and steals from right under your nose.

When Satan Gets Your ATM Card

So for the remainder of this chapter, I want to speak specifically about what happens when satan gets your ATM card.

I want to talk about what happens when satan gets license in your life. No one can just walk up to any bank or ATM machine and demand that it gives them the money from someone's account.

They have to be given license. They have to have a card, a number and the key ingredients necessary to steal that money from you. It is the same with the enemy.

He cannot walk into your life any time that he pleases and just start attacking you. It does not work that way. He has to be given license. He basically needs you to walk up to him and say, "Here devil. Here is my ATM card and here is my PIN code. Go ahead and draw out as much as you would like."

So we are going to look specifically at how satan is given license and then we will learn how to snatch that card back, get a new one, and take that license away from him.

GET RID OF YOUR NORMAL

It is not only possible to take away satan's license, but it is easier than you think. The problem with many believers is that they are so used to the attacks of the enemy that they start to think of it as normal.

They say, "We get sick at this same time every year. It is normal." Perhaps, you get an unexpected bill and the taxes go up again. You say, "Well, that is just how it is."

You may come into a nice lump sum of money and then someone gets sick and you have to use that money to buy medicine. You think, "That is just how it is. It is normal."

Then you are driving home late at night, you do not see a car in front of you and then you bump into his bumper. You say, "Oops. These kinds of things always happen." No. These kinds of things should not happen to a believer.

God has called us to walk in His divine blessing. When these things happen in our lives, there is one reason for it. Satan has license in your life. You do not have to accept his attacks, his theft on your finances, sicknesses, money being stolen from you, relationships being destroyed, strife in your home, or people being hurt.

> **KEY PRINCIPLE**
>
> The enemy can't just walk into your life any time he pleases and attack you. He has to be given license.

You do not have to accept these things. These are all signs that satan has license in your life and he is attacking you. You do not have to lose things anymore. You do not have to have things break on you anymore.

WE'RE NOT GONNA TAKE IT!

If things are frequently being broken, it is a curse of destruction and you do not have to accept it. The first step to dealing with the enemy is realizing that you do not need to take it.

How stupid would I have been if I never called the bank and I just let that person continue to steal from us? You would look at me as if I was crazy. Yet, how often do you allow the enemy to walk through your life and do whatever he wants in it?

You allow him to destroy what he wants to destroy, and to steal what he wants to steal. Then, you say, "That is just the way that it is." No. That is not the way it is. Your first question should be, "Is this a blessing?"

If it is not a blessing, then it is not of God. I do not know about you, but when there is something that is not of God, I do not want anything to do with it.

However, we become a little phlegmatic. If it is not a blessing, then you do not have to take it anymore. The reality is that satan has license in your life right now. So, let's find out how satan was handed your details on a silver platter and then let's learn how to take them back.

A Dirty 3-Letter Word

Here is the three letter word that always gives satan license – sin. This nasty, dirty word that no one wants to hear is the thing that gives satan license in your life. However, people like to think of themselves as victims.

They want to think that they were just walking along and satan just attacked them for no good reason. No. He has to be given license. If satan could attack anybody at any time that he wanted, then the Church would not have survived past the first century.

Sure, he can apply pressure from the thoughts, circumstances and the world, but it does not mean that you have to sit and take it. You can rise up and overcome those things. Sin gives satan license in your life.

Make a nice, big list of all your problems in your life right now. Now, next to each one, write – SIN. It is your sin, that is the open door. Nobody wants to hear that.

No one wants to hear that satan has license in their lives because they messed up.

Yet, when you get that conviction, it is such a relief. Do you know why? As believers, we have a solution for sin. Actually, we have a five second solution. It looks like this, "Father, forgive me."

Just like that, you are cleansed, the sin is gone and the door is closed. Satan has no license anymore. However, you are still walking around saying, "That is just the way things are. The devil is at it again."

While you walk around saying that, the devil becomes this big monster that you cannot overcome. Your struggle becomes a problem that you cannot solve.

After some time, you will think that you are never going to overcome the problem. That is why when you get the conviction that sin has given satan license, it is a relief.

KNOW WHICH SIN IS SIN

> *James 4:4 Adulterers and adulteresses! Do you not know that friendship with the world is enmity with God? Whoever therefore wants to be a friend of the world makes himself an enemy of God.*
> *5 Or do you think that the Scripture says in vain, The Spirit who dwells in us yearns jealously?*
> *6 But He gives more grace. Therefore, He says: God resists the proud, but gives grace to the humble.*

> *7 Therefore submit to God. Resist the devil and he will flee from you.*

It is a relief because we have a solution for sin. We have something that we can use to deal with that, which means that we have a solution for the problem.

Let's take the example of a man struggling with sexual sin. Which statement below do you think would give him hope?

"You just have to fight the works of the enemy and resist temptation, because the enemy has chosen to always attack you with these thoughts."

"You are responsible for your own sin and if you can remove the license you gave the enemy, you never have to struggle with this attack ever again."

The one statement creates a victim. The second gives a solution. It leads them to the blood of Jesus, because to take away the license they must put their own sin under the cross.

And so, I am going to speak about some of the main things that give satan license. Sin is a very broad subject. Just because you have a bad thought does not mean that satan is now going to come and steal all your finances.

It takes a bit more than that. If you accidentally let a bad word out this morning, that is not going to give satan license to steal in your life. Those are not the sins that I am talking about. We all fail and make mistakes.

HEART SINS

The sin I am speaking about here is the sin that opens your heart to the enemy and gives him license in your life. We have spoken in detail about the battlefields of the enemy.

Now when the enemy has been throwing thoughts of fear at you and you succumb to it, you engage him in warfare. The greater sins are not the mistakes we make as we fumble through life, trying to decide what is right and wrong.

The sins that give the enemy the greatest license lies in this passage

> *Ezekiel 14:3 Son of man, these men have set up their idols in their hearts, and put before them that which causes them to stumble into iniquity. Should I let Myself be inquired of at all by them?*

Our hearts are what the enemy is fighting for, because when he has our hearts, we are fighting for him, against God's plan. So many look at the sins of the flesh, without realizing that if the idols of the heart had not been worshipped, the flesh would never have had reason to fail God.

> **KEY PRINCIPLE**
>
> The sins of the heart are what gives the enemy the greatest license. When satan has our heart, we end up fighting for him, against God's plans.

It is your pride that leads you to dominate others. It is your selfishness that leads you into bitterness when you do not get your own way. It is your own fear of lack that leads the way to the love of money and uses it as an idol.

It is the guilt that you entertain that leads you to hide your sin and do things you would never do. It is the cravings that strive within you, that when entertained, give satan the ground that he needs.

When you entertain the temptations, you build an idol in your heart. This idol is what gives the enemy all the license that he needs to attack you. James tells us in the passage above, that when you succumb to the world and allow it to control you, put yourself at enmity with God. Well if you are not fighting on God's behalf, but against him… exactly whose side are you on here?

I taught in much detail how the enemy gains license in my teaching *The Stain of Sin – Overcoming Curses* so I do not want to labor on the teaching aspect here.

Rather, I want to challenge your flesh and your thinking. I want you to realize that each time you entertained that temptation to become bitter, that you gave satan ground in your heart. Each time that you decided to do things the world's way, you handed satan your ATM card.

You gave him license in your life, by putting yourself at enmity with God. Does this nullify the blood of Christ? Not at all – you just need to give God the control again.

1. BITTERNESS

> *Hebrews 12:15 Looking carefully lest anyone fall short of the grace of God; lest any root of bitterness springing up cause trouble, and by this many become defiled;*

Bitterness is a poison dart with the power to cut through your armor. Not only does it pierce your heart, but poisons your spirit until you are paralyzed.

Just by entertaining bitterness you take a hammer to your own castle walls and invite the enemy in.

The greater danger though, and one not many people realize, is that when you are bitter against someone, that you establish a spiritual link with them!

Although your feelings are negative, the person you are bitter towards is on your thoughts. They are influencing your emotions and have a hold on you!

Where this is tricky is in situations where that person really did do something bad and hurt you. I challenge anyone not to feel bitter if they were abused. That is the hardest part of all and I do not think that anyone would stand as judge because the enemy tried to destroy you through someone else's wicked actions.

However, whether your anger is justified or not, while you keep your bitterness toward that person intact, you are no longer a victim. You are putting yourself under their bondage. Why bitterness is so difficult to deal with, is because you are often bitter for a reason.

WHEN IT HURTS

Jesus had every reason to be bitter. All He did was pour out everything He had. He gave out His life, love, and time. He hardly ate or slept, and when He did try to get a few winks on a boat, He was woken up to save everyone. What did He get in return?

Soldiers dragged Him into their camp, stood in a circle around Him and ripped His clothes off.

Then, they took a staff and hit Him on the head with it. They pushed a crown of thorns into His scalp and beat Him in His face, pulling out His beard. As if the physical injury was not hurtful enough, they did not relent from making fun of Him and laughing at Him.

Jesus did not get bitter.

Do you still think that the offense you experienced is not possible to forgive?

Did He deserve to have disgusting men spit in his face? His rebuff through sweat and pain was, "Father, forgive them. They do not know what they are doing."

If any man could have been bitter, it was Jesus. The thing is, had He retaliated in anger, He would have played right into satan's hands.

> **KEY PRINCIPLE**
>
> By entertaining bitterness, you take a hammer to your own castle walls and invite the enemy in.

Now I am not saying this to be callous. I am saying it to set you free. It does not matter what that person said or did to you. It does not matter how intense any abuse may have been.

Your bitterness will ensure that for the rest of your life, they have control over you. As long as you hold onto your bitterness, they keep you under them. They keep you submitted, rejected, afraid and condemned.

For as long as you are bitter, you submit yourself to that person and you remain under their bondage.

Rather deal with the bitterness and say, "Father, forgive them. They do not know what they are doing."

When you do that, it will set you free. Once you have dealt with that bitterness, you can say, "Father, forgive me for being bitter. I let it go Lord. You are there to vindicate me and cover me from now on. I want to come under your hand and not under this bondage.

You can see it as a big package being put onto a boat and shipped out to sea. When you deal with your bitterness, you will truly break those links and be free in ways that you cannot imagine. From there, healing can begin, perhaps for the first time.

Have you tried to receive healing for the same hurt over and over again? Healing cannot begin until those spiritual links are broken. You can only break them once you let that bitterness go. Burn that umbilical cord in the spirit and start walking a life of victory today!

2. Fear

> *Romans 14:23 But he who doubts is condemned if he eats, because he does not eat from faith; for whatever is not from faith is sin.*

Fear is to faith as water is to fire. It neutralizes it! Not only does fear give your sound mind to the enemy, but it also disassembles your "faith weapon." Succumbing to fear gives the enemy license over your soul, which will lead you into many wrong decisions.

Here is the catch though. There are many who will label anger as a sin. They will call lust and greed sin. There are not many who will call fear sin. Think about it though. What is the one thing that pleases the Father? The Word says that without faith it is impossible to please Him.

Fear is the complete opposite of faith. What you do not realize, is where you allow fear to grip you, it is in that moment, you have more faith in satan than you do in the Lord Jesus.

Let that sink in for a moment.

What is fear? I am not talking about reverential fear that is borne from a respect towards the Father. I am talking about fear that grips you. Let me give you a helping hand here.

WHICH FEAR IS YOURS?

Fear has many faces. Try to identify yours. Are you afraid that you will not make ends meet at the end of the month?

Are you spending all your money on self defense because you are afraid that you will be attacked?

How about your health? You get a little cough and run to the doctor because you are afraid of getting cancer?

Fear has become such a part of your life, you do not even realize it. You fear that people will reject you. You fear that you will not get favor. You fear loss of your possessions and positions.

Fear, fear, fear… it is such a part of your life you do not even realize it. You rationalize it calling it, "Common sense." Well it seems to me that what we call "common sense" in our day and age, Apostle Paul and Jesus both labeled as "lack of faith." As this passage says so beautifully in Romans, "Whatever is not from faith is sin."

Fear is simply faith in satan's plans instead of faith in God's power. You fear loss more than you believe in the gain God has promised.

You have more faith in satan's threat to attack you, than you believe in divine protection.

You have more faith in the fact that you will get sick than you believe God's word for healing.

I am driving this point home hard, because as a prophet you have no place in your heart for fear. Not only does it neutralize your faith, but it does something much more damaging than that.

It spreads like leaven into the lives of others. Each time you minister with a spirit of fear compelling you, you impart fear and not faith to God's people. You undo the very thing you were called to do.

KEY PRINCIPLE

>Fear is simply faith in satan's plans
>instead of faith in God's power.

You commit ministry suicide by pouring our darkness instead of light. None of us want to imagine that. We want to hope that we equip the body of Christ. We want to imagine that we are the drill sergeant that teaches the Church to fight effectively. We do not want to think that we are responsible for corroding the armor that they do have.

Identify the fears that satan has used to cripple your faith. Your faith is right inside. Get rid of the hindrances and watch God's promises come to life!

3. OBLIGATION (GUILT)

> *Romans 13:7 Render therefore to all their due: taxes to whom taxes are due, customs to whom customs, fear to whom fear, honor to whom honor.*
> *8 Owe no one anything except to love one another, for he who loves another has fulfilled the law.*

Contracts and binding vows belong to God alone. Even in the Old Testament it tells us not to "vow anything" to man. In fact, Solomon tells his son that if he ever made such a vow, to get out of it as soon as he could!

So there are things we owe and things that bring us into bondage. For example, according to Romans, we owe honor to some, and respect to others. We owe honor to those in the Lord, who have helped us along our journey.

We owe respect to our fathers and mothers and to our leaders. At the end of it though, Paul tells us to owe no man anything, but to love him.

Now, there is a certain obligation that turns into bondage, especially in family relationships. A bondage where you feel obligated to make up for all they did for you. A place in your life where honor given turns into a string of controlling circumstances that cause you to pay for what you received at the cost of the call of God on your life.

This is very common in parental relationships, especially when your parents paid a great price to raise you. You feel like Elisha when the call comes.

You say, "I cannot leave my mother and father. I must bury them." This is what Elisha said to Elijah.

Elisha was saying, "I cannot just leave my parents." That obligation could have cost him his prophetic call. Even Jesus said, "Leave your mother and father and sell everything that you have and come and join me. Let the dead bury the dead."

He was very strong in His statements, because you cannot be motivated by obligation. It is a negative motivation and it does not produce faith, hope, or love. When we respond out of love, it is not an obligation, but a joy.

When I go and spend the entire day shopping to find you a special gift for your birthday, I think to myself, "I cannot wait to see their face when they get this gift for their birthday."

It is exciting. I go from place to place to find the perfect thing and I spend a fortune on it. Then, I come and give it to you. I am not giving it to you out of obligation - I am giving to you because I love you.

However, if your birthday comes up and I say, "I suppose I better do something. I guess this is what they want. Let's go and do it." Then, you start dragging through the stores and you finally find something after who knows how long and you are doing it just to keep your mom happy because you know that you will never hear the end of it, if you do not get her something.

If you do that, you just lost your reward. That bondage is going to destroy you, because that is obligation. If you cannot do it in faith, hope, and love, then do not do it at all because it does not add to your life, it simply keeps you in bondage.

The enemy loves to play on it because you feel so guilty and condemned. You think, "They have done so much for me and what have I done?" The decisions that other people have made, are the decisions that other people have made.

So you live your life for the pleasure of others instead of the pleasure of God. So who is your master again?

> **KEY PRINCIPLE**
>
> Anything you do, if under obligation or guilt, you are allowing satan to steal from you.

If your parents (or anyone else for that matter) gave up something for you, it was their choice.

You can appreciate it, love them for it and thank them for it, but you cannot spend the rest of your life paying them back for it.

It will come in the way of your call and what God wants to do. The Word is clear. It says, "Owe no man anything. Do not make vows." You cannot pay them back.

How horrible would it be for me, after I have found you this precious gift and given it to you and then you reach in your back pocket, pull out your wallet and say, "How much do I owe you? I have to pay you back."

How insulting! When I do something in love, it is not to get a return. Your parents' reward is in their giving. I did not give birth so that my children could pay me back for the hours of childbirth! My reward lay in the moment they opened their eyes for the first time and looked into mine. The first smile. The first step. The first, "I love you, mommy," was all the reward I needed.

They have already received their reward because they desired to see you rise up, and so you did.

That is their reward. In addition to that, they can expect the Lord to reward them. If someone poured into you because of your call, the Word says that when they did it to you, that they did it unto the Lord as well!

You cannot remain under obligation. You need to go and fulfill the call that God has for you now and not let the enemy keep distracting you.

This is a huge open door and if you are battling with generational curses, really look at this. It is satan's way of keeping you trapped. It is a really subtle one because you do feel obligated because they did something amazing for you. You feel compelled.

When God tells you to give or to do something, by all means, do it. However, do it with the right motivation. Do it in faith, hope, and love. Then, you are transmuting into your heavenly bank account, and you are pouring out into God's economy.

Yet, when you do it under obligation, you are allowing satan to steal from you. It is completely counter-productive.

4. Disobedience and Rebellion

There is no better way to handing over your rights than by disobeying your commander-in-chief. If two generals, each of a different army were to tell you (as a soldier) to follow an order, whose order would you follow?

It is logical to assume that you would follow after the General whose army you are enlisted in! If you followed the orders of the opposing general, the world would call that treason.

Well the bible has another word for it. It calls it a spirit of rebellion. Witchcraft.

> *1 Samuel 15:23 For rebellion is as the sin of witchcraft, and stubbornness is as iniquity and idolatry. Because you have rejected the word of the Lord, he also has rejected you from being king.*

When you deliberately choose to disobey the Lord and follow the instruction of the enemy, you put yourself on a dangerous ground. Not only do you remove yourself from the Lord's covering, but you come under the enemy's control.

None of us would like to think that we do that, but think again. Think back on the last time the Lord gave you a direct order. Think back to Adam and Even. Allow the words to echo in your mind, "Of this tree... you shall not eat."

Have you ever pondered the following passage?

> *1 John 5:16 If anyone sees his brother sinning a sin which does not lead to death, he will ask, and He will give him life for those who commit sin not leading to death. There is sin leading to death. I do not say that he should pray about that.*
> *17 All unrighteousness is sin, and there is sin not leading to death.*

What is John talking about here? He is talking about deliberate sin. The kind of sin where God tells you to go left and you go right. The kind of sin, where your King tells you to take the land and destroy all of the sheep and goats and you keep them instead (AKA King Saul).

As believers, we are covered by grace, but sometimes you use that grace as an excuse to skirt around the direct commands that God has given to you. Now I am talking about a lot more than just a deliberate disobedience of the Word. I am speaking of direct rebellion against something that the Lord has told you to do.

Obviously, if you commit adultery, you are in direct disobedience to the Word of God! However, what about if God has told you to move to another city, or to give something up that would cost you something?

The love and grace of Jesus is a constant. So much so, that even after Adam and Eve's rebellion, the Lord made a way for their redemption. That did not save the garden for them though. It did not stop the curse from creeping in and stealing the blessing that they had become accustomed to.

CONSEQUENCES TO SIN

The same applies to you. There are many who take the grace of God for granted. Their thinking is, "When I am done sinning, I know that the grace of God will be waiting for me. The blood is there any time I need it. So I will just do this 'one thing' and return to the Lord. He will understand."

I am sure that Jesus will understand. Much to our own shame, His blood is indeed there once you are done running. However, in the process of your rebellion, how much ground did you give over to the enemy – or did you forget that you are at war?

> ***KEY PRINCIPLE***
>
> When you deliberately choose to disobey the Lord and follow the instruction of the enemy, not only do you remove yourself from the Lord's covering, but you come under the enemy's control.

Do you think that if you open up yourself wide for the enemy that he will let you go? You are a prophet! Saint or sinner... he knows who you are now. Do you really think that he will let it go?

Have you noticed how the warfare has suddenly increased in your life as you have received a conviction of your call? Why? The open doors were always there, prophet! Satan always had that license, but he is choosing now to use it.

He was waiting until your bank account was nice and plump before emptying it. Why waste your time in an empty account? Why waste time on someone who is no threat? Why waste time on someone that will undo themselves anyway?

However, the more you rise up, the more the enemy is looking for. So what you got away with in the past, you will not get away with now.

So after looking at all the battlefields, you realize that the greatest enemy is not the one from without, but the one that strives daily within us!

Like I said before, there is a simple solution to this license that the enemy has gained in your life. It is a little shuffle that I like to call the three-step.

LET'S DO THE THREE STEP!

> *James 4:7 Therefore submit to God. Resist the devil and he will flee from you.*

Confess. Submit. Resist

How much blood will it take to cover your sin? His blood was enough to cover the man who crucified him. It covered Peter's blame for renouncing Him and the sin Paul carried throughout his life each time he thought about how he assisted in the stoning of Stephen.

Stoned anyone recently? Well if the blood of the Lord Jesus could cover them, it stretches far and wide enough to cover yours. There is no sin that you cannot bring to the cross.

Once your conscience is clear before the Lord, you can walk into the Throne Room with boldness. While your heart is still condemning you, you will avoid the Lord.

Confess

Not only that, because your sin has you fighting in the wrong camp, you will find yourself fighting against the hand of God. Confession removes the veil. It smashes the idol you have built in your heart that was constructed by your excuses and logical reasoning.

Jesus taught His disciples to pray and included, "Forgive us…" How often do you repent? How often should you repent? Personally, I am so used to the sight of the cross, I try not to count the times I confess my sins, cause my diary would be overflowing. How long does it take? How much effort?

Yes, it does not take much effort to confess sin – the effort comes in admitting it! Admitting sin means admitting defeat. Confessing sin admits to the beam in your own eye, which somehow negates the splinter in your brother's.

Confession is a risk. You risk losing your pride. You risk losing face. It could even be…Lord forbid… that you are wrong! It's strange how many excuses we will hold on to, to not feel ashamed or wronged.

But I am talking to a prophet… you should be used to being wrong by now. You should be used to false accusation. In fact, you should have sipped on false accusation for breakfast, snacked on wrongful treatment for lunch and dined on injustice just before bed!

Hey, this is old hat to you. So why do you find it so hard to confess sometimes? Perhaps it is because you feel that you are pulling your heart into the open – baring it, in vulnerability. Perhaps it is because you are so angry and every cell of your flesh wants to see that person pay the price for your vindication.

Whatever it might be… this is the first step toward taking back your ground. Confession is key. Without admitting your sin, you will not get the orders you need from your General.

SUBMIT

Once your sin is out of the way, you can approach the Throne of Grace. If you try to approach the Throne before confession, your eyes will not be clear enough to see. Your ears will be filled with so many voices that you will not hear with clarity.

However, once you come humbly before the Lord, your sin neatly pinned to the cross, you should be at peace. There is no greater feeling than a recent crucifixion. (Something only a prophet would say.) Because in this moment, everything becomes really quiet.

In this moment, you can hear a pin drop in the spirit. Now is the time to submit. To bring yourself back in line with the Lord's will. It does not take long. Actually the longest part of the process is admitting your sin.

To get a conviction of your sin is the toughest part, but once you see it, submission is a natural result. In fact, nothing in this world could hold you back from running frantically to the Throne Room so that you can throw yourself at the feet of the Father!

Now that you are in line with what God wants and you are sure you are hearing His words and not your own hurts and fears, you are ready for the final step.

RESIST

You better believe it! Once the scales have fallen from your eyes, you will begin to see how the enemy has been using this open door in your life to wreak havoc. You will see how much damage your anger has wrought on your relationships.

You will see how you have broken lives through your submission to lust. You will look up one day to see your children estranged because of the deep-rooted bitterness you allowed to fester there.

When this conviction comes, there is nothing in this world that will stop you from putting the devil in his place. Sure, you might have fallen prey to his ploys, but he is still the one that brought about that destruction. You do not need to accept this theft any longer!

Now is the time to remove the license from the enemy that you have given to him and to take your land back.

The Three Step in Action

So how does this look practically? I have given you a lot of explanation here, but let me write out how it might look practically. Of course you will have your own words and your own sins to contend with.

Say then that the Lord has exposed a deep bitter root in your heart. A bitterness that has given the enemy a huge advantage on the battlefield!

> "Lord Jesus I see this bitterness in my heart. Lord for so many years I felt so justified. You saw what they did to me. You saw how much I hurt. Jesus you see how much I need healing.

Regardless though, I cannot afford this bitterness.

It has become an idol in my heart! It has become something I have clung to for so long now and I want to bring it to you. I bring it to your altar and I leave it there. I smash it Jesus and ask you to forgive me. Forgive me for not walking in love. Forgive me Jesus for holding on to this anger inside instead of onto you.

I submit myself to you right now. I give you license in my life Lord and I ask for your wisdom. Show me your plans. Show me your love. Let me see this person through your eyes. I want to see as you see!

Now satan, I remove this license that I have given to you right now. You have played around with it long enough. I rebuke you and tell you to leave right now. You take all your curses with you and every last influence on my life. Every thought of anger you keep putting in my mind!

I call every circumstance into line according to God's promise! You will no longer try to 'pull my string' to make me angry any longer. I will not fall for your ploys. Now be gone in Jesus name!"

It does not take long to overcome. It does not take long to remove the license that satan has gained in your life.

CHAPTER 09

HOW SATAN GAINS LICENSE THROUGH OTHERS

Chapter 09 – How Satan Gains License Through Others

Every Christmas I make a traditional South African treat called "koeksisters." They are a sweet dough that is rolled, plaited and then deep fried. As they turn golden brown, you take them from the oil and then submerge them into a cold spicy syrup. Every year I have to make a double batch, because this syrupy treat is gobbled up in no time!

If you want to make sure that the fried pastry drinks up that syrup, you have to make sure the dough is nice and fluffy. That means leaving the dough for at least an hour to allow the yeast to work through it. It is fascinating to watch that dough double in size. Simple flour and egg is transformed into fluffy goodness with just a bit of yeast in the batch.

In this illustration you find the secret to how the enemy gains license through others in your life.

I have spoken in some detail about how the enemy can only attack when he is given license through sin. So then, why does the attack come when you know that there is no sin in your heart?

Or is there? Come now, you should know by now that I am not going to leave it at that. A challenge is most certainly forthcoming! It is true, there are many in this world only to happy to live sinful lifestyles. There is nothing new under the sun and even Paul and Peter spoke of sin in every shape and size.

I have included quite a lengthy passage here, but I want you to take some time to read through it, before you move on to my next point.

> *1 Corinthians 5:7 Therefore purge out the old leaven, that you may be a new lump, since you truly are unleavened. For indeed Christ, our Passover, was sacrificed for us.*
> *8 Therefore let us keep the feast, not with old leaven, nor with the leaven of malice and wickedness, but with the unleavened bread of sincerity and truth.*
> *9 I wrote to you in my epistle not to keep company with sexually immoral people.*
> *10 Yet I certainly did not mean with the sexually immoral people of this world, or with the covetous, or extortioners, or idolaters, since then you would need to go out of the world.*
> *11 But now I have written to you not to keep company with anyone named a brother, who is sexually immoral, or covetous, or an idolater, or a reviler, or a drunkard, or an extortioner—not even to eat with such a person.*
> *12 For what have I to do with judging those also who are outside? Do you not judge those who are inside? 13 But those who are outside God judges. Therefore, put away from yourselves the evil person.*
>
> *Galatians 5:19 Now the works of the flesh are evident, which are: adultery, fornication,*

> *uncleanness, lewdness,*
> *20 idolatry, sorcery, hatred, contentions, jealousies, outbursts of wrath, selfish ambitions, dissensions, heresies,*
> *21 envy, murders, drunkenness, revelries, and the like; of which I tell you beforehand, just as I also told you in time past, that those who practice such things will not inherit the kingdom of God.*

So what does all this talk of sin got to do with demons? Plenty actually. Take a look at 1 Corinthians 5. What is Paul talking about here? He speaks of the "leaven" that has the potential to influence others.

In comes my "yeast" illustration. Jesus told the disciples to be careful of the "leaven" of the Pharisees. This is what I am going to show you right now. I am going to point out the leaven that satan has been using in your life to gain ground on each battlefield.

Contamination – How You Partake of Leaven

At the core of this teaching is what I simply call "contamination." In other words, when someone else is walking in sin, it is possible for you to become contaminated by their sin. It means that because they have given satan license in their lives, you can share in that oppression by partaking of their leaven!

Now like I said, there are a couple of things that cause us to take on the "leaven" of others. This means that if someone else is living in sin and willingly giving satan the run of their lives, it is possible for you to share in that!

Now there are a number of ways that you can open your heart or share in someone else's sin. I am going to expound on each here, but before I do, I want to make a point that I am going to highlight.

> **KEY PRINCIPLE**
>
> Regardless of the sins of others, you remain responsible for what you submit to. The devil can knock at your door, but you are not a victim if you open it and let him in. You just made that sin your own!

In other words, even if you opened your heart to someone with a spiritual bondage, let's be honest, you did so because of needs or desires of your own heart. You are responsible for your own spiritual health. You cannot call yourself a victim and say that you are experiencing warfare because of "someone else's sin."

Experiencing a backlash? Well then break spiritual links! Experiencing external attacks from prayers being sent your way? Then raise your shield.

What are you here, a warrior or a mommy's boy? Stop messing around with the devil and stop messing around with your pity party and raise the sword God gave you.

The moment you took hold of that sword you stopped becoming a victim and were appointed a warrior. Sorry prophet… no time to bleed for you. No excuses for you. No pity parties and certainly no excuses.

Think I am being tough? Then please, feel free to put down your sword and be a pew warmer. No? I did not think so…

You are called to be a victor and if you cannot even rise up and take control of the realm of the spirit in your own life, what hope do you have for the Church? If you continue to see yourself as a victim of warfare all the time, what message of faith do you have for the Church?

"Come and let me show you how to look defeated?!"

How about we say, "Come let me show you what the hordes of hell look like as they run off in seven directions!"

> **KEY PRINCIPLE**
>
> Regardless of the sins of others, you remain responsible for what you submit to. No one is a victim.

Now that's what I am talking about! You pumped? Good, then let me show you just what tactics the enemy has been using to bring about external oppression in your life.

(Remember I taught on external oppression at the beginning? If you cannot remember that part, please review it, because this is the warfare that you engage in for most of these points.)

1. CONTAMINATION THROUGH SPIRITUAL LINKS

> *1 Timothy 5:22 Do not lay hands on anyone hastily, nor share in other people's sins; keep yourself pure.*

If you open your heart and establish a spiritual link with someone who is "sinning unto death", what they are giving license to will effect you. Say for example there is someone that is willingly submitting to lust and has a pornography problem.

If you open your heart to them through prayer, it would not be surprising to find yourself under the same bondage. This is especially true in ministry when you are pouring out.

Yes, there is a lot of teaching in the church about how you can receive contamination by people praying over you. Yes, this is true and when you open your heart to receive an impartation from that person, if they are in bondage, you will share in that leaven.

However, because this is a book for prophets, I want to switch it up. Keep in mind that when you pray for others and open your heart to them, if you do not follow through, you will find yourself contaminated!

If you partake of their sin or even condone it, you share in it. That means if there is any demonic bondage in their lives, you will experience the same attack.

Have you ministered to someone and gone from there only to get into an accident, get sick, or have nightmares?

When I pray for someone that has a contamination in this way, I see it like an umbilical cord that a baby has with its mother. What the mother eats, the baby feeds on.

Now when you make such a spiritual connection with someone that has deliberate sin, or demonic bondage in their lives, you are being influenced by it!

Breaking Spiritual Links

Now before you get frantic and in your paranoia hold back from ministering to others, let me just make this simple.

In the same way that the link was established, you can also break it. It takes seconds. What is the greatest way to overcome any curse? To curse back? No, the Word says to bless and curse not.

> **KEY PRINCIPLE**
>
> If you partake of someone else's sin or even condone it, you share in it. That means if there is any demonic bondage in their lives, you will experience the same attack.

Breaking spiritual links is so simple. "Lord Jesus I speak blessing on my brother. I pray that you will take the word I shared and bring conviction to their hearts. I also break spiritual links with them Lord. I let them go and put them into your hands. Amen."

It's that simple. Do you know what keeps the link in place so tightly? Trying to be their Holy Spirit! When you make yourself responsible for their change and their spiritual walk, you stand in the way of their relationship with the Lord.

Only the Holy Spirit can convict. Now as prophets... we are big softies. We see someone who is hurt, and in bondage, and we want so badly for them to be free.

TRYING TO PLAY "HOLY SPIRIT"

You want them to experience Jesus face-to-face. You want to see that gaping wound in their hearts healed. So you travail long. Now there is nothing wrong with that. However, you go to bed that night, still struggling.

You call them the next day. Follow up. Run after them... wanting so badly for them to "get it."

Careful now, because satan just pushed you beyond what God intended. Answer these questions for me.

   a. Did you minister what God told you to minister?
   b. Did you show them the love of Jesus?
   c. Did you base your revelations on the Word?
   d. If you did none of the three above, do you at least love them with the love of Jesus?

If you can answer yes to any of those questions, then the Holy Spirit has something to work with. You see, you might have linked to them... but they linked to you too! They might have bondage, but you have a little bit of leaven of your own! You got a whole lot of anointed healing and power in your spirit!

You did your part. They opened their heart to you, did they not? They received your ministry, did they not? Then say your piece and get out of the way! Allow the Holy Spirit to finish what He started. It is not your job to try and force that person to change now!

Did I just hear you say, "oops" in the spirit? You would not be the first prophet to run so hard, that you ended up running over the person you were trying to help. Just learn from that now, because you can only take so much spiritual warfare – why call more onto yourself?

I NEED THIS SO BAD!

Another way that you keep those spiritual links in place is when you have not allowed the Holy Spirit to take you through your prophetic training properly. If you have been through the *Prophetic Boot Camp* book, you will have read about how much the Lord will deal with your needs and the striving within.

He does this, because you cannot afford to have your need for love and recognition met in others! When you do, you hook up an umbilical cord and you are feeding off that person!

You are feeding off their love, allowing it to fill you up – instead of allowing the Lord to be your Savior.

You are the servant to that which masters you. Who is mastering you right now? Where do you go to "feel good about yourself?" Where do you go to get your "love meter" filled up?

When you feel insecure or upset, where do you go to feed? Well whatever (or whoever) you are feeding on, is entering your spirit. You better make sure that it is from streams of living water, and not a muddy puddle.

So if you are ministering to others, just so that you can hear the words, "You are wonderful! Thank you so much! You are amazing…" You are in some dangerous water.

If you have a need to minister, and a need to give, you are establishing spiritual links with people that you really should not be. Are you bold enough to tell me that you do not "need" to minister?

Oh good, then you would not have a problem with not counseling, ministering to someone or giving them a prophetic word for a month? I tell you what, why don't you just sit in your prayer closet with Jesus and not even say a word to anyone else?

Still think you do not have a need to minister?

Ministry should always be a pouring out. If the tables are turned and you are going to "get" something from that person, know this... you are partaking of their leaven.

Do you still think that you are a victim of spiritual warfare? Is the source of your warfare from someone in your life that is in bondage? Then let me challenge you further. Let me ask you these two questions:

a. Are you "hanging on" and trying to get them to change – playing the Holy Spirit?
b. Are you needing the love and acceptance from this person so bad, that you go to get something instead of just to give?

2. Sexual Relations

> *1 Corinthians 6:16 Or do you not know that he who is joined to a harlot is one body with her? For the two, He says, shall become one flesh.*

Saving yourself for the wedding night has become a rare commodity in today's age. The Lord knows I questioned this myself. Sex, is like any other sin right? So if I swear or have sex before marriage, aren't they the same?

The problem is seeing sex as just being a sin. The blood of Jesus can cleanse us from all unrighteousness. What the world (and many believers) do not realize is that the sexual act outside of marriage is not just all about "sinning."

Perhaps you already know this, but if not, allow me to switch on the light for you.

The Sexual Act is a Covenant Act

The act of marriage does a lot more than just use your body for sin. When you perform the sexual act, you perform a covenant act. Do you remember when Abraham made a covenant with the Lord?

There were specific acts that they followed. There was a shedding of blood and a time when each person in the covenant gave all they owned and who they were to the other. This is quite a full subject, so I am going to give you the bottom line here.

Abraham killed the animals, but he also withheld nothing from God – even his own son. The Lord reciprocated and did not withhold His own son! A covenant was made with the shedding of blood and sharing of lives.

Do you see this? Ever wondered why the Lord made it why a virgin has a hymen and often bleeds during her first intercourse? What is that all about? It is because the marriage act is part of a covenant!

When you are married, you give all you are to the other person. On the wedding night, you shed blood and the covenant is sealed. Even in the world, a marriage is not established until you have had that wedding night. The sexual act seals the covenant.

Sex is a lot more than just a physical release. It is an act that joins you to the person that you are submitting your body to (just like it says in this passage above in 1 Corinthians).

Now whether you performed the act willingly or unwillingly, the act itself establishes a spiritual connection.

Looking for the source to a spirit of lust or uncontrollable desires that keep attacking you? Then start making a list of your sexual encounters.

I have seen the enemy try to destroy so many prophets with this even before they realize their ministry. Child abuse and promiscuity are not uncommon amongst those who are called to serve the Lord. Surprised? You should not be. If there is one thing that has the potential to steal our humanity from us, it lies in the realm of sexual abuse.

Of course if you had many sexual partners throughout your lifetime... you have a lot of spiritual links to deal with! This is even stronger in the case of previous marriages. The two have been made one!

Consider the consequences of your actions for a bit. For everyone you have had intercourse with, you joined your spirit to them. Now if your spouse is the only person that you have ever had this relationship with, you are in good standing! However, if you have had many... you have got some repenting and spiritual link breaking to do!

Isn't interesting that Paul says that when you fornicate, that you sin against your own body? In other words, when you engage in sex outside of God's order, you are opening the door for the enemy to attack! You are bringing damage to yourself. The Lord does not need to punish you, you punish yourself through your sin, by giving satan license in your life.

3. SPIRITUAL IMPARTATION

> *2 Timothy 1:6 Therefore I remind you to stir up the gift of God which is in you through the laying on of my hands.*

Timothy had it easy! Paul paid the price and he got to eat the fruit of that labor. He did not even need to strive for the gifts. Paul, having been the way ahead of him, simply imparted them to him.

> **KEY PRINCIPLE**
>
> There is no greater way to share in both the anointing and contamination of someone else than through the process of spiritual impartation.

Unfortunately for us, we have a "drive-through" society that goes around as little orphans begging on the street corner of every revival.

Let a man of God show just a bit of power and a line will form outside his door for people hungering for a "touch of power." They want the impartation. They crave it, thinking that along with it, will come a reality of Christ.

Christ is the anointed one. You want the anointing? Take hold of Christ. How many spiritual fathers did Timothy need to get a couple of gifts? Just one. If you look at how the Lord brought them together and used them as a team, you see a very specific relationship.

Can you imagine Timothy doing the rounds between Peter, Barnabus, and good old James? Weren't all these men anointed? Well people were healed by their shadow, so I think that they had a bit of power in their lives.

Looking at the New Testament, it is a no brainer. So then, why does the Church not follow the example of Timothy? Instead, we have a "seeker friendly" church, seeking God through the laying on of hands and an instant impartation of the anointing.

FITTING THE ANOINTING

Firstly, that anointing came at great cost to the person that is walking it out. You are a prophet - you know what I am talking about here! Imagine a special agent who went through intense training to make him the best of the best. He is then rewarded with a medal from his country.

That medal is but a picture of his journey. It is the same with the anointing. To walk out the anointing on your life, you had to become the kind of person that could walk that anointing out. How can that be handed out to just anyone?

Could you pin a medal of honor to someone who enlisted yesterday? Yet is that not what is happening in the church today? As if the anointing is a bag of candy to be handed out. Have we forgotten who the Anointed One is?

So if someone comes along to "receive an anointing," but they are not the kind of vessel that can walk it out, what are they getting?

You open your heart wide to receive everything from this man of God, but if you are doing so unled, what exactly are you picking up here? The Holy Spirit is the one who anoints. If He has chosen not to anoint you through this man, what are you receiving?

All you are getting is a spiritual link to everything else that is in their spirit. Is it any wonder that some of the greatest bondages in your life come from those you received impartations from? You opened your heart and spirit wide to receive. However instead of receiving a gift like Timothy got from Paul, you got a whole lot of leaven.

4. DOCTRINE

> *Matthew 16:12 Then they understood that He did not tell them to beware of the leaven of bread, but of the doctrine of the Pharisees and Sadducees.*

A prophet in deception perhaps releases a spiritual force, but a teacher in deception builds a foundation on which people build their lives. It is for this reason that doctrine is second to impartation when it comes to giving satan license in your life.

It is because doctrine shapes our view of Christ. It is the telescope through which we understand the Lord and what He wants to do in our lives. It revolutionizes our souls!

Building blocks of doctrine shape what we think, how we feel, and how we walk out our salvation. If you had never heard that you needed to repent of your sin, you would not be born again.

WHY DOCTRINE INFLUENCES

If you had never heard that Jesus could heal, you would not ask Him to heal you. Doctrine is intensely spiritual because it shapes the convictions of your soul. As you have already learned, the soul is your control tower. It determines whether the flesh or the spirit gains dominance.

Now what if the doctrine you have learned puffs up the flesh? Now let's add another twist to this. What if the person laying the foundation of that doctrine is contaminated?

What if the bricks they are building with are dripping with poison? You already know that you release what is in your spirit through words and actions.

So what then, if their words were tainted with what is in their spirit – which is spiritual contamination? Now someone could be teaching good truth. They could even be teaching moral and solid principles. However, I ask you this, "What is the spirit behind that teaching?"

You are allowing your soul to be shaped and built a brick at a time through this teaching – the bricks might look good – but what about the spirit that is contained within them?

So I am going to bypass obvious heresy here. I think it stands to reason that if you allow yourself to get swept away by every wind of doctrine, and get bound up in heretical teaching, that you are giving satan free reign in your life.

> **KEY PRINCIPLE**
>
> Because doctrine shapes our view of Christ, it is second to impartation when it comes to giving satan license in your life.

I want to talk more about teaching where the teacher had some serious demonic bondage in their lives. Has the Lord been calling you to get rid of old books and teachings?

You might look at them and wonder to yourself, "What is so wrong with this?" Perhaps nothing. It could be that the teaching itself is good, but perhaps you are not looking deep enough here.

There could be two reasons that the Lord is telling you to get rid of old doctrines.

The first, is that the doctrine served its purpose and is now standing in the way of something new the Lord wants to lead you into.

The second, is that although the doctrine itself was all right, the teacher's spirit was contaminated and this is what the Lord wants to displace in your life.

I will say this for dealing with contamination through doctrine – it takes time. It takes a lot more than just "breaking spiritual links." It means having your mind renewed as Paul tells us in Ephesians 4:23.

It means displacing the old with the new. Finding new teaching to displace the old with.

5. Prayers Sent Against You – Friendly Fire

There is power on our tongue. Whether saved or unsaved, man has a spirit. Sure, the spirit of someone that is unsaved is dead to the Lord. This does not mean that they do not have a spirit though.

Consider the incredible things that man has been able to accomplish. We have built bridges, made dams, and sent people to the moon! You learned in *Prophetic Functions* about the spirit of man. It holds power.

Now when you get born again, that spirit is renewed and your spirit is combined with the Lord's. That is what this passage means,

> *John 15:7 If you abide in Me, and My words abide in you, you will ask what you desire, and it shall be done for you.*

There is power when we get born again and allow the Lord Jesus to abide within us. In fact, we have enough power to move mountains, and call those things which are not as though they were!

As we allow ourselves to go through the fire and let the Holy Spirit strip things from us that hinder that anointing, it increases. Your words will carry a greater authority as your faith increases and as you go through the process.

That is why I labor the point of praying only as God leads. Why? Because when you send out a word in the name of the Lord, you are releasing a force into the earth.

I could not believe my ears when I heard about a military term called "friendly fire." It is a nice way of saying, "We accidentally dropped a bomb on our own men and killed them."

Friendly fire is alive and well in the church and with every arrow that you send forth from your flesh, or inspired from the enemy, you are releasing a force.

> *Isaiah 54:17 No weapon formed against you shall prosper, and every tongue which rises against you in judgment you shall condemn. This is the heritage of the servants of the Lord, and their righteousness is from Me, says the Lord*

Words are weapons! When the person speaking them has some spiritual authority, that weapon is sharpened. It is a sad state to see an army stop in the middle of warfare to shoot arrows at one another instead of taking the enemy out. Sometimes we do the devil's work for him.

By praying against someone's will, or forcing our own ideas on them, we release a spiritual force all right – but which side of the camp does this force come from?

If you are not praying with the leading of the Holy Spirit, then who is leading your prayer? Are you sending forth arrows of life and hope, or poison tipped darts that the enemy can piggy back on, to wreak havoc in the lives of others.

On the Receiving End

Now I am not going to lie – you will be on the receiving end of those poison darts more than once during the course of your ministry. In fact, expect it! You are not going to keep everyone happy in the church. Sometimes your message will upset people.

There are times when you will be led to another country, or to leave your home church. People will try to "help" by praying their own burdens over you.

Many call it "witchcraft" and "cursing." I am not so sure that I want to be as harsh, because regardless of what they pray, you still have a choice.

When people pray against you, it gives satan license to bear pressure on your circumstances. It gives him the "in" that he needs to start sending some bombs your way. He might choose to attack your mind with thoughts. Your circumstances might begin to bear on you.

Personally when people are praying against me, I feel it like a dark cloud. I feel like I am walking in mud and fumbling everything that I try to do. Now all of this attack has a single purpose – to get you to give in!

The enemy is just hoping that you will get angry enough to entertain bitterness. Now if he can get you returning some "friendly fire" of your own, he can stand back and watch the fireworks. No need for him to waste any of his resources when he has you doing his job for him.

So what is the solution here? There is a weapon that is powerful for pulling down strongholds. Check it out.

> *James 3:9 With it we bless our God and Father, and with it we curse men, who have been made in the similitude of God.*
> *10 Out of the same mouth proceed blessing and cursing. My brethren, these things ought not to be so.*
>
> *Luke 6:27 But I say to you who hear: Love your enemies, do good to those who hate you,*
> *28 bless those who curse you, and pray for those who spitefully use you.*
> *29 To him who strikes you on the one cheek, offer the other also. And from him who takes away your cloak, do not withhold your tunic either.*

Satan Gains License Through Others

So does this mean you just sit idly by while others curse you? Hardly! I am telling you to pick up a weapon that will neutralize every license that the enemy has received, and then turn the tables on satan.

> ***Key Principle***
>
> Love is the greatest force of all, so how about using it as a weapon? Speak blessing and pray for favor on the those who are praying against you?

How about instead of getting angry and throwing out some poison darts, you speak blessing on the person and pray for favor instead?

Returning the Fire

It would be so easy to "send the arrows back" or to judge them, but why do it the hard way? You and I both know that love is the greatest force of all, so how about you learn to use it as a weapon?

Get into the Throne Room of God, allow the love of Christ to fill your spirit and then you send out a deadly "love arrow" that will cover the multitude of sins that have been sent your way.

Understand me clearly here, love is not passive. People think that to love your enemies is to just sit and "take it." To many, loving someone else means just welcoming the abuse and then in saccharine sweet tones saying, "I choose to forgive you brother."

Give me a break! I really do NOT want to "forgive you brother" and I am really not going to take this attack. I tell you what I am going to do – I am going to love you to death. I am going to do a lot more than forgive your "friendly fire." I am going to douse it with so much love that you cannot stand.

Now we are talking! This is the kind of warfare that the enemy has no weapon for. The Word says that the enemy cannot comprehend love – so why fight fair? Let's pull out weapons he does not have. Follow the lead of your Savior. Jesus bled all over his enemies and reached out to sinners. Time we learned to do the same.

6. PRAYING UNLED

Faith pleases the Father. If someone does not reach out to the Lord in faith, He will not reach back. It's tough though when you see someone going through a hard time. You see them struggling in their marriage, or with a physical problem.

Every prophetic bone in your body wants to heal the broken-hearted. Sometimes our fire can lead us beyond what God intends. Sometimes we jump in too early. We jump in before the person had a chance to cry out to the Lord.

When did the Lord send Moses to the Israelites? It was when they cried out to Him. Now the Lord is just awesome – even before they cried out, He was already making a plan.

He had his agent going through weapons training in the courts of Pharaoh, and learning wilderness survival skills on the backside of the desert.

All He was waiting for, was for them to cry out. You saw what happened when Moses jumped in too soon! He killed that Egyptian and the very people he tried to save, tattletaled on him!

There is nothing quite like the timing of the Lord, so do not rush in until you get the call, because if you jump in ahead of time, you will get the same welcoming committee that Moses did!

I taught you in some detail about the essentials of intercession in the *Prophetic Anointing* book. Review it if you do not remember the principles.

Know this – when you jump in to pray being motivated by your emotions, not only will you be ineffective, but you are begging for a backlash!

If you try to deal with a demon that someone else is not ready to give up, you will find yourself under that attack. You do not know the condition of the person's heart. For all you know they are deliberately sinning and their struggle is the consequence of their "sin unto death." The scripture I used at the beginning of this chapter reiterates what I am saying here.

If you pray unled, you step out into the open field for the enemy to attack. This holds true of spiritual warfare as well.

Just because you have learned all of these principles, does not mean that you run onto the battlefield and pick a fight with the devil.

Did the enemy pick a fight? Then by all means, please remind him whose land he is standing on.

Did the Lord lead you into spiritual warfare? Then arm yourself and take on the hordes of hell.

Having a bad day and just in the mood to punch the devil? Eat some ice cream, drink a coffee and go for a walk until your head clears. No king in his right mind goes into battle just because he is having a bad day. He has a clear goal and intention.

The King of Kings has a clear intention as well and it is for you, as a prophet to have your ear keenly pressed to the ear of His chest to hear the thunder of his heartbeat.

RISE TO THE CHALLENGE

When the thundering sound echoes through your mind, and your spirit is ignited with faith, you will see the battlefield ahead of you. You will look down to see the sword in your hand and you will face the enemy of the Church.

You will see him charge and you will not be moved. You will look up to see his archers poised to attack you with those poison darts. They will not move you. You will smile and calmly step forward to remind all present that you stand by the blood of the Lamb and the word of your testimony.

We need not fear the work of the enemy, because while he is running around trying to get license through our sin and the sins of others, we have a secret weapon hidden behind our shields.

We have love that renders any dart useless. We have faith that can push back any flood, and hope that keeps us so focused that no demon in hell can trick us into obeying anyone else than our Lord.

Prophet of God... it's time to start a revolution. You know all the enemy's plans now. You can see his tricks. Now I have just one question for you. What are you going to do about it?

Wallow in your sin? Complain about injustice? Excuse failure because of the prayers of others?

How about you just take up arms and do what you were called to do – to undo the works of satan and take this land back for our King!

CHAPTER 10

OUR POSITION IN CHRIST

CHAPTER 10 – OUR POSITION IN CHRIST

> *Ephesians 2:2 In which you once walked according to the course of this world, according to the prince of the power of the air, the spirit who now works in the sons of disobedience:*

The princes of the air control the systems that bind us. They block our minds and divert our paths. They have power. They have authority. They have the say.

Well… that was the reality two thousand years ago. From the moment that Jesus lived a sinless life and revoked every last authority satan had gained in this world, the earth and all the territories were given back to their rightful owner.

Unfortunately, the inhabitants of the earth did not get the message. Some were only too happy to enter into the new covenant, while others remained under the control of the enemy and his hordes. As we revisit Ephesians 2:2 you understand some of what Paul is saying here.

There is no doubt, that within his realm, satan has power. However, there is just one little point that we often fail to see. This world and everything in it, is no longer deeded as part of his kingdom! It belongs to the Lord and His chosen ones.

Tell me prophet of God, are you a chosen one? If so, then the blood of Christ seals the covenant that gives you authority in this earth.

Now it is not your fault that so much of humanity has not yet gotten the memo. We continue to pray for the evangelists to go forth and to save the "prisoners of war" that satan keeps captive. The unsaved that continue to live and act according to the course of this world.

> **KEY PRINCIPLE**
>
> There is no doubt, that within his realm, satan has power. However, we hold the authority in this earth whether satan gets his way or not.

However, just because they are under the princes of the air, does not change the facts. The fact that this earth belongs to the Lord and the redeemed.

You see, we hold the authority in this earth whether satan gets his way or not.

What I want to smash in this chapter is the concept that the devil can jump on you at any time that he wants, but I also want to bring you to a conviction of your victory in Christ.

TOO DEMON CONSCIOUS

I think sometimes we get too demon conscious in the church - especially if you have been in deliverance ministry circles. You end up seeing demons everywhere. You imagine them jumping all over the place, and in and out of people.

Before you know it, you are telling people to be careful because there is a demon here, and a demon there. You stub your toe or have a bad day, and you put it down to being spiritual warfare.

With all of this going on, you get so focused on the devil that you forget that you have the victory in Christ.

You forget that at the name of Jesus every knee will bow and every tongue will confess that our Jesus Christ is Lord. You forget to stand and say, "No satan. Today you are not getting your license. Today, I cancel and suspend it!"

Where Demons are Limited

It is very easy to get caught up in looking for demons and finding demons. Let me tell you, if you are looking for demons all the time, they will be only too happy to oblige – anything that will take your eyes off the Lord.

Yes, we have been talking about dealing with demons and dealing with open doors, but you never have to feel like a victim.

So dump the idea that demons are just jumping from person to person without any provocation – as if they could do as they pleased. Consider this passage below. Jesus confronts the man with a ruler demon called Legion and casts it out. Look at what happens next.

> *Luke 8:32 Now a herd of many swine was feeding there on the mountain.* ***So they begged Him that He would permit them to enter them. And He permitted them.***
> *33 Then the demons went out of the man and entered the swine, and the herd ran violently down the steep place into the lake and drowned.*

The demon asks permission for himself and the hordes under him to be allowed to possess the swine. What does this tell you about the limitations of the devil? He cannot just go ahead and possess anyone that he wants to!

Jesus had to give them permission. Only then could they take the swine on a joy ride. There is a misconception that if someone has a demon cast out of them, that it will just jump on to the next person, as if the demon is a flu virus!

No, demons need license! They need to be allowed to possess and they must be given a key for entry. No one can just be possessed by a demon without that demon having been given the authority.

So you cannot say, "Shame, this poor guy was just walking along and a demon jumped on him, and now he is demonized." No, satan was given license. The good news? As believers, we have the authority to take that license back.

Singling Out the Victim Mentality

That means that you do not need to be sick. You do not need to have things breaking all the time. You do not have to struggle with your finances and have things stolen from you.

You are not a victim! You are in Christ. Because you are in Christ, you are part of the solution. You can overcome any demonic work in your life.

When we smash this victim mentality that the church has, we can start seeing some victory.

There is no hope when you teach that "satan can get you" anytime that he wants to. By thinking like a victim, you are already defeated.

You think, "Well, that is just what happens to us in our family. Finances, blessing and joy are not things that I get. Other people walk in favor and get blessed, but not me. That is not my portion."

> **Key Principle**
>
> You are not a victim. Because you are in Christ, you can overcome any demonic work in your life.

If you are thinking like that, you have a victim mentality. For as long as you think that way, satan will continue to have license in your life, because let me tell you something – Jesus Christ is not a victim.

Satan had the Lord beat up, crucified, and even scattered His disciples, but did the Lord Jesus sit there at the feet of the Father saying, "Woe is me. I am defeated. Satan beat up on me"?

No. He rose from the dead in His glory, sat at the right hand of the Father, and said, "At my name, every single one of you powers and rulers will come under my feet. I now have dominion over you."

He did not sit and grovel under satan. I like that Jesus was so bold and arrogant. He was so sure of Himself that the Word says that He walked right into the pit of Hell and took back those keys of life that satan stole from Adam right back in the beginning.

He snatched them and said, "Give me back those keys."

UNDERSTANDING WHAT JESUS DID

> *Revelation 1:18 I am He who lives, and was dead, and behold, I am alive forevermore. Amen. And I have the keys of Hades and of Death.*

You already know that you give satan license when you walk in disobedience. Nothing depicts this more than the first sin ever committed in the Garden of Eden. Still sinless, Adam and Eve walked in close fellowship with the Lord, having the world at their fingertips.

That was, until that fateful day when Even wandered close to the tree of good and evil. The Lord had not forbidden the tree of life. They could eat of that as much as they liked. However, the Lord Himself wanted to be their guide. He wanted them to receive from Him, and to be pure in their intentions.

Was it the tree of good and evil that defiled Eve, or the fact that she disobeyed a direct command that the Lord had given? In that moment, she did a few things. Firstly, she disobeyed the Lord. Secondly, she obeyed the voice of the enemy. This was the greater sin.

It could well be that Adam and Eve were not yet ready for the tree of good and evil. They were new to the life and the world that was around them. They were getting to know the Lord, one another, and their place in the Universe. Above all the Lord, like a tender mother, was raising them and teaching them from His own hand.

I do not doubt that a time would have come for them to learn for themselves, however just like a baby first learns to talk like its parents, so the Father was raising His first children by teaching them what was right and wrong – right from His own mouth!

The Price of Sin

The moment Eve ate that apple, her knowledge started to come from outside the Lord, and clearly, she was not ready for it. Not only had she sinned, but a rush of knowledge flooded them both, and that began to separate them from the Lord, and one another.

They sewed fig leaves together to hide their nakedness from one another. Their sin not only brought a separation between them and the Lord, but it gave satan just what he wanted – the gift that the Lord had given Adam and Eve, the earth.

The Genesis 1:28 says that the Lord gave Adam dominion over the earth. In other words – he was set as the ruler of the earth. The earth was his to subdue and command! By obeying satan, Adam and Eve handed that dominion over.

So, for a long time, Adam became the victim. Fortunately for us, the story did not end there. The Lord made a plan. He said, "Let me make a second Adam - One that will face the same temptations from the devil, but that will not sin. I will raise up a second Adam that will obey my voice instead, and so take back the dominion that man lost."

And so entered… Jesus! Jesus came along and said to man, "No more! You will no longer have to battle under the slavery of the law or of this flesh. You can have the victory."

From the moment that Jesus stormed into the throne room of the enemy over two thousand years ago and snatched those keys back, we also received that authority as well, because the Lord did not take those keys to hold onto them.

He gave the keys to us!

Do you not realize that you hold in the palm of your hand, the keys of life, of death, and of Hell? You can overcome any work of the enemy.

Your battle was won two thousand years ago. I know that you have heard this preached time and again, but there is something invigorating being reminded of it.

You see, warfare tends to get a bit tedious, if you keep going into it too much. You start to think that your day should be filled with fighting the enemy. You start thinking that you have to struggle with the enemy.

STAND!

> *Ephesians 6:13 Therefore take up the whole armor of God, that you may be able to withstand in the evil day, and having done all, to stand.*

The greatest victory that you will receive will not be when you break spiritual links with someone, or bind the enemy in your life. The victory is found in the last two words of this scripture. To stand.

When you do that, you do not stand in the authority of Colette Toach, because Colette Toach does not have authority in this earth. However, Colette Christ Toach has authority in this earth. Why? It is because I am in Christ, and He is in me.

I am a warrior standing on the battlefield, and from every side, they see but one thing. For miles around, the enemy sees my armor gleaming as a flash of fire in the sunlight - the blood of Christ having stained every inch of it, covering my sin, and covering my works.

It strikes fear into the heart of the enemy, and as I raise my sword with a flash of lightning, the demons flee.

When I stand up and speak to the devil, he does not see me. He sees the blood of Christ that was shed two thousand years ago. He has a dramatic flashback of Jesus storming into his throne room and scaring the life out of him and taking those keys back.

Unfortunately, we have forgotten to stand in the blood and in the authority that God has given us. You keep spouting off your prayers and stomping up a cloud of dust in spiritual warfare – all in of your own strength. God does not need you to do a rain dance. Want to send the demons running? One word in Christ is all that it takes.

> *Deuteronomy 32:30 How could one chase a thousand, and two put ten thousand to flight, unless their Rock had sold them, and the Lord had surrendered them?*

You can send a thousand to flight with one word in Christ. When you get the conviction that satan has no authority, you will no longer think or respond the same way.

You will say, "What are you doing on my land? Who invited you? I do not even care who invited you, because I have the authority to revoke any invitation. Get off my land!"

You will start to feel a conviction and power build up inside of you. This is the goal of prophetic warfare.

A Revolutionary Conviction

You need to realize that at the name of Jesus every knee will bow. All things in heaven, in earth, and under the earth, must bow to His name. All you need to do, is get into Christ.

However, you are too busy "getting in there" and doing warfare that you do not realize that you are not just the pawn in the chess game - you are the king. You can stand and let the others do the work.

You have a whole legion of angels at your command. When you speak the word into the earth, they will do the warfare on your behalf. However, you are like a little pawn that tries to raise his sword and take on the entire hordes of Hell all by himself.

If you are doing this, you are doing it without the Lord's help and you are playing solo. That is one surefire way of getting your butt whipped. Why go onto the battlefield unarmed and without marching orders?

This is why you keep getting overrun by the enemy. Stop and realize that you are seated in heavenly places with the Lord Jesus.

SEATED IN HEAVENLY PLACES

When I am seated in heavenly places, it is like standing on top of a very tall hill and I am looking down at the battlefield knowing that I have an entire legion at my disposal. It brings perspective to look down and see satan way down at the bottom. All that is left to do is to say, "Get out of here."

> **KEY PRINCIPLE**
>
> When you have a clear conviction of your authority and victory in Christ, it surpasses everything else.

When you have a conviction of your authority and victory in Christ, you do not even have to break spiritual links anymore because it is done. You will say, "I do not care what authority you have been given, I take it back. I do not care who has given you license, I block it in the name of Jesus and you will loose your hold."

It surpasses everything else. It is a place of maturity, rest, and of authority. The Lord Jesus looked at those demons and told them to go into the pigs, and they went. This is the same authority that you have been given.

You need to come to a place where you are seated in heavenly places, and you are looking down at your problems, instead of up at your problems all the time. When you do that – your problems will move.

Establish a Favorable Battlefield

> *Mark 11:23 For assuredly, I say to you, whoever says to this mountain, 'Be removed and be cast into the sea,' and does not doubt in his heart, but believes that those things he says will be done, he will have whatever he says.*

When you stand, armed, and in faith, you already have the victory over anything satan puts in your path. Any mountain. Any circumstances. Any attack from the system. Any sin. Any person. Any demon.

Do you understand? There is an easier way! Why work yourself up for hours trying to beat the enemy up on his home ground, when you can rise higher and speak from a perspective of authority?

So often you run headlong into the enemy's camp, trying to engage him at his strong point. Do not be foolish! Even the world knows that if you want to defeat an enemy, the best way to do it is on your terms. When you draw them onto the battlefield of your choice – you have the upper hand.

The day Jesus died on the cross and covered you from head to toe in His blood, He gave you that upper hand. He instituted a battlefield upon the mount of Golgotha.

You already learned about the battlefields that the enemy has. He fights you in your soul. He attacks through circumstances and through the systems of this world. This is his "happy place." (If one could ever imagine the devil being happy!)

So why fight in a way that is comfortable for him? He has been strategizing for thousands of years, so why give him the satisfaction of engaging on his terms?

Take the battlefield to one of your choice. Draw it from your mind and engage from Golgotha. From there, you can overcome every work of the enemy.

> **KEY PRINCIPLE**
>
> For it is when you stand crucified in Christ and speak covered by the blood of Christ with faith in your heart, the very kingdom of the enemy will be torn apart.

Often though, you are too busy staring at this huge mountain that satan has put in your path instead of getting up there and looking down at it and saying, "Hey mountain, get out of my way. You are bothering me. Get off my land. Move it."

When you are seated in heavenly places and you have a conviction of your authority, you do not doubt for a minute that victory will come to pass. It is back to the principle of prophetic intercession that you have already learned.

You need to get back to standing in your authority. Realize that you already have the victory. I do not care how much you have sinned or who has spoken curses over you. When you stand in faith and authority, that mountain must be moved.

Those arrows that have come at you must be stopped. With one word they will indeed be stopped, if you know your authority in Christ.

BLOOD. NAME. VICTORY.

> *Colossians 2:13 And you, being dead in your trespasses and the uncircumcision of your flesh, He has made alive together with Him, having forgiven you all trespasses,*
> *14 having wiped out the handwriting of requirements that was against us, which was contrary to us. And He has taken it out of the way, having nailed it to the cross.*
> *15 Having disarmed principalities and powers, He made a public spectacle of them, triumphing over them in it.*

BLOOD

Your sin gave license to the enemy in your life. The sins in this world have given satan license to bring pressure on you through circumstances. The systems of this world, giving satan so much glory, bring pressure on you.

Each license that a prince of darkness is given, signs a command for attack. This attack is destined to trip you up and to bring you to the point of surrender. He lobs fear at you. He puts pressure on you through financial loss and accusation.

Your knees become weak. You become aware of your guilt, fear, and bitterness, and it begins to rise in your heart. It is a battle you feel you are losing. In the moment that the world feels as if it is on top of you, is the moment for you to understand Colossians 2:13.

Satan might be able to get license through sin to attack, but there is a way to get past that. The blood.

Your Crowning Moment – the Cross

Prophet of God, don't you understand yet why you had to face the cross all the time during your training? Have you not yet grasped the power that Christ is trying to impart to you?

You have seen the flesh that needs to go. You see the sin that must be repented of. You have understood the character in you that needed to be shaped by the mighty hand of the Holy Spirit.

What you have not seen is that when you are identifying with Christ on the cross, you stand in the greatest victory you have ever known. In that singular moment, you are untouchable.

> **KEY PRINCIPLE**
>
> How often should you be going to the cross? You should never get off!

That is what Colossians is talking about here! When you are identified with the cross, your sins are not seen! Satan no longer has anything to attack you with! He has no grounds and there is no curse in hell that can alight on you.

So tell me prophet of God, how often should be going to the cross? Just until you reach prophetic office? Once a day?

I say this with all conviction – you should never get off!

Did you truly think that the travail you went through was just for punishment? No, it is on the cross that you find true power. When your sin is covered by His blood, in that moment realize that it is Jesus who has the real power.

In the moment you are nailed to that cross, Jesus descends on His white horse, with sword in hand. Like a Goliath of God, He steps out and obliterates Lucifer and his hordes of hell.

All that the Lord is waiting for right now, is for you to give Him license.

NAME

Where is our authority vested? It is invested in Christ and on the finished work of Calvary. It is not invested in your works. It is not even invested in your repented sin. Your authority will become a reality when you realize that it is not by might or by power that you fight – but by the Word of God!

Your authority lies in the fact that Jesus made a show of the enemy. Do you see what verse 14 says in the passage above? It says that when you are in Christ that the ordinances against you are blotted out!

Every little decree that satan has written about you, because of your sin, or the sins of others – is neutralized! His blood is fire to every contract and signed declaration against you.

The secret? Stay under the blood. You know that the blood has power. The whole Church knows that. Yet so many misunderstand it. When something goes wrong, they "plead the blood" over and over again.

For goodness sake Church of the Most High, would you please stop pleading the blood and just get under it? Take hold of it and put your sins under it! Give the Lord license in your life through repentance, and start speaking forth His Word.

Then you will see things happen. Our authority does not come from saying the right words. You can say, "I plead the blood" Or "In Jesus Name" a hundred times and get nowhere in the spirit.

It is not about the words you use, but the authority behind those words. When you use the name of Jesus with a full conviction of His promises and the reality of your righteousness, then you have something to work with!

Victory

When Jesus descended into hell and stormed in on satan, He took his power over you away. It is like satan was sitting there with this nice, big shotgun taking shots at you. Jesus walked in there, stole his shotgun, and all that was left was this weeny, little man that had nothing left to do. The enemy is powerless.

The problem is that you see the devil and curses as such a bid deal. You see demons as an overwhelming attack. You say, "The spiritual warfare is so intense."

In three days, Jesus took down satan's entire kingdom! He is powerless. The only time satan is given power is when you give it to him.

Not only did Jesus take the power away from satan, but He gave us power over satan. He said, "Here is a lion and I have taken out its teeth. Here is a shotgun, deal with him as you will."

Yet, you keep seeing satan as a big, roaring lion. You make the mistake of thinking that you have to press through for hours in travail and warfare.

THE WARRIOR RISES

If you are experiencing warfare after warfare in your life, there are open doors there because satan cannot walk in whenever he wants. If you have dealt with the open doors, and there is still warfare, then you have not risen up in your authority, because satan is a defeated foe.

> *KEY PRINCIPLE*
>
> The only time satan is given power, is when you give it to him.

Have I got my message across yet? Satan is defeated! You hold the key to victory in the palm of your hand. You can decide to tell him what to do.

If satan thinks that he has an in, we can go to the Lord and submit ourselves to Him and then say, "Oh really devil? Did you really think it would be a good idea to walk into my life right now and mess with me?

"I do not come to you as myself or with my good intentions, great ideas and what I feel is right. I come to you in the name of the Lord Jesus Christ. I come in His blood and you will bow at His name and you will get your hand off my circumstances and you will get yourself off my land!"

Does that ignite a fire in your belly? I know that it does, because you are a prophet. It burns in you to level the devil.

Prophet of God, you have the authority over the smallest demon all the way up to Lucifer himself.

Suspended on the cross, dead to your sins. Armed with the power of the blood. Fighting with the sword of faith, with a strong hand of authority. Prepare yourself devil… there is a prophetic warrior on the battlefield.

CHAPTER 11

WEAPONS TRAINING IN AUTHORITY

Chapter 11 – Weapons Training in Authority

There is a reason that not everyone signs up for military training. In most countries, it is not mandatory for you to sign up. In those countries, people have a choice and you will notice that not everybody enlists.

Why is that? It is because military training is hard work. There is nobody that is born knowing how to go to war and defeat the enemy.

We got my son a toy sword and he thought that it was one of the coolest things ever. He went around with his sword, beating up his sisters and even getting me as well, from time to time when I was not looking.

It is all fun and play, but if he were ever put in a real war situation, he would not last five seconds. Right now it is just fun for him. If ever a time comes where he wants to become a real warrior, it is going to take some training.

Yet, somehow, prophets have this strange idea that different rules apply in the spiritual realm. They think that just by being called, they are going to wake up one day and will just know how to engage in spiritual warfare.

They imagine that a mantle is going to come upon them and they will just get words of wisdom and know exactly what to do. Sorry to break the news to you, but spiritual warfare is hard work. It takes some training.

You Need Training

It means that you are going to have to take your spirit, soul, and body and put some training in there. Ready for some push-ups?

Consider the chapters before this as schooling. You have learned the tactics and have come to an understanding of the principles to engage. However, you need a bit of spiritual muscle.

It is one thing to know how a sword is made, and another to pick it up and use it!

> *Hebrews 4:12 For the word of God is living and powerful, and sharper than any two- edged sword, piercing even to the division of soul and spirit, and of joints and marrow, and is a discerner of the thoughts and intents of the heart.*

The writer of Hebrews knew a little bit about the power of the Word. He called it a sword, a weapon of war. Have you ever tried picking a sword up?

When you watch the movies, it looks so easy. You just pick up a sword and do some fancy footwork. However, anyone that knows anything realizes that it takes some training to learn how to pick up that sword.

I love this description because, in this passage, we are given many elements of truth.

Firstly, we realize how powerful and sharp the sword is. Then, we have to stop and realize that if we are going to use this sword to go into warfare, we better learn how to pick it up, to stab, block, and plan the next step… all at the same time!

I know that prophets hate it when I say to them, "It is going to be hard work." Sorry guys, if you want to make it to prophetic office, there is no such thing as a shortcut.

If you want to enter into spiritual warfare effectively, there is one tool, one weapon that you will want more than anything. That weapon is the Word of God.

WEAPONS OF WARFARE

I have taught you a lot on defensive warfare. I taught you how to block and how to get the enemy out of your life.

Each of these principles have taught you to stop the enemy from attacking you.

In many ways, I have helped you identify where the enemy has gained license in your life and to close that door on him. Unfortunately, it is like closing the door after the enemy has already gotten in.

The time has come for you to do a lot more than close doors. The time has come to learn how to deal with the damage that he has done.

This is a common mistake that many people overlook when they are learning about the concept of giving satan license. They realize that satan got entry into their lives through sin.

They experience a curse like sickness, and the principles help them see where the enemy got into the camp. A huge crack is made visible in their spiritual walls. They see that through their bitterness, that they have allowed the enemy to keep attacking. So they close the door right away. They repent and deal with that bitterness.

The struggle continues. Why? Well you closed the door, but did you kick the devil out? Taking away the license of the enemy will stop him from getting in again, but what happens once he is already in your camp and is setting your life on fire?

Well then, we need a little bit of one-on-one with the devil and remove him forcibly from our lives. Welcome to offensive warfare.

SPIRIT AND WORD

> *Jude 1:20 But you, beloved, building yourselves up on your most holy faith, praying in the Holy Spirit,*

Now this is going to take some effort, but fortunately you are already halfway there. Remember the *Prophetic Anointing* and everything you learned about the Spirit in *Prophetic Functions*?

By learning to flow in revelation and coming into the reality of the anointing is half of your training. However, standing in the spirit is not enough. You might be able to see in the spirit and speak with the anointing, but without faith behind all of that, you will not make a dent in the enemy's armor.

Prophets can often make this mistake. They think that just because they see a demon in the spirit, that it will go away. Do you have the authority to tell it to go? Do you know without a doubt that the enemy will leave when you tell it to?

Revelation is not enough. Revelation is like standing on the battlefield and seeing the enemy through binoculars. You see where he is attacking and where his weak points are. It tells you where to attack, and how to attack.

The anointing is a force of power behind you! It lifts you up and gives you the strength to engage. Now what use would any of that be without a sword? What are you going to do? Go onto a battlefield with a dagger, or a broadsword?

The anointing might empower you… but what weapon do you have for it to empower? A dagger might be empowered greatly, but it is still only so big! You will have to do a lot more work to take your enemy down.

If you want to do some real damage out there, we need to work on your weaponry. I do not doubt you can see the devil. I do not doubt that the anointing will strengthen your arm. How about we just put something of worth in your hand to fight with, huh?

SHARPEN YOUR SWORD

Pick up your sword, prophet of God. Pick up the Word! The Word is living and powerful. It is not just a bunch dead words.

Now the effort I am talking about here is not just picking up the scriptures and reading a couple of chapters each day.

The Word has a personality and life of its own. When you can take that life and feed it into your spirit, and discipline your spirit and your mind with it, you are going to start becoming a dangerous warrior.

> ### KEY PRINCIPLE
> The reason why your anointing and your authority is lacking, is because you do not have enough living Word inside of you.

Have you been wondering why your warfare lacks the edge? Why is it that you have to speak ten times before the devil listens? Something happens, and then you face warfare through circumstances and you do not overcome easily - you have to really push and fight.

In this moment you should realize that your level of warfare is not quite where it should be.

The reason why your anointing and your authority is lacking, is because you do not have enough living Word inside of you.

BUILDING YOUR OWN STRONGHOLD

If you do not put it in, it is not coming out. You cannot just read the Word - you have to study the Word. This means learning, memorizing, and pushing the Word down into your spirit.

You may say, "I read ten chapters a day. I read the Word all the time." It is not good enough to just read it.

Reading must give way to understanding, and then give birth to wisdom. The Logos word must make way to Rhema. Essentially, you have to feed it into your mind, emotions, and will.

You already learned how satan tries to bring the battle to your soul. He revels in setting up camp in your mind to prick your emotions, and seduce you into sinful action.

Not only are you going to learn in the rest of this chapter, how to defend yourself from such an attack, but you are about to realize that transforming this battlefield will tip the scales in your favor.

It is not good enough to just set up good defenses, you need to begin constructing your own strongholds with which to level the gates of hell and his kingdom.

MIND

> *Romans 12:2 And do not be conformed to this world, but be transformed by the renewing of your mind, that you may prove what is that good and acceptable and perfect will of God.*

Whipping your mind into shape is the easy part. By meditating on the right words and pictures, you begin laying a foundation from which your emotions can begin to gain momentum.

For you to defeat the enemy, you need to believe that you can defeat them.

KEY PRINCIPLE

What soldier steps onto a battlefield not knowing if he will win? A defeated soldier.

Do not step onto that battlefield until you know without a doubt that you will overcome. Do not think that you can just start attacking the enemy and "figure it out as you go." You are just asking for a backlash.

Stand in faith, and satan cannot touch you. Here is the thing though - do you believe that you have this authority? Well there is only one way to make sure that you are fully armed for this: get your mind in gear. Your mind needs to be made up.

Unfortunately, you may have a lot of bad experiences to work through. You have suffered loss and fear. You have felt the sting of rejection and struggled with sickness. Poverty, hurt, and failure have left scars in your memory to the point where you know you should have faith, but still think at the back of your mind, "What if…"

Those pictures need to be changed. When a difficult situation comes at you, your reaction has to change. Do you want to know where you need to build some spiritual muscle?

Its easy. What is your "point of weakness"? Which circumstance always causes you to react? In *Prophetic Boot Camp*, I went into this in detail! What is your "trigger"?

Like I already shared, mine was a fear of financial lack. Because of all the experiences I had in life, they had left a deep scar that had built up over the years. All the enemy had to do was tweak a few circumstances, and instead of responding in faith, I responded in fear.

What is your weak point? Which circumstances bring the worst fears and thoughts out of you? Once you know that, you then know where you must begin.

Pick up the Word and begin feeding it into your spirit. Now when I say "feed it into your spirit" I do not mean just read it.

If you want to begin to see the truth according to the Word instead of according to your circumstance, it means using the language of the spirit to get that scripture into you. The language of the spirit is one of types and shadows... pictures!

If you want to change the way you think, take the scriptures and visualize them. In our Pastor Teacher School, I teach my students to "live" the Word. The Lord taught me to do it in a fascinating way, and I do not think that just pastors and teachers can benefit here.

He had me experience the living Word. As I read the Scriptures, He had me close my eyes and imagine myself right back in the past when it was written. He told me, "Imagine now that you are walking through the marketplace with Paul as that demonized girl followed after him.

Can you hear the shouting in the marketplace? It is dirty and dusty, and your feet are dry. You feel the stones under your shoes as you walk and feel the dry wind on your face.

There are different smells. Some pleasant – some not. There are some selling brightly colored cloth. Paul is on a mission. His eyes are not turning to the left or right. He is completely focused. He does not notice the fruit basket that just got upset. He is engaged in conversation and the girl behind him keeps interrupting, distracting him from his conversation…"

The more I read the Word by living the Word, the more the Word abided in me and me in the Word. These pictures started to change the way I thought. I began to gain so much more than just authority through this process. I began to develop a love relationship with the Word by experiencing its personality.

The nature of Jesus came to life for me as I strained through the crowd towards the cross, or felt the dust fall on my head as the roof was removed for the lame man to be let through.

THE STRONGHOLD BLUEPRINT

Each of these pictures began to lay a foundation in my mind. This is what the Word means when it says that we should have the mind of Christ. In other words, we need to think like Jesus. How else can you do that than by allowing the Word to renew your mind?

When the promises and reality of the Word is more of a reality to you than what is around about you – you just put the blueprint together for a stronghold.

Not only will your mind become protected from the enemy's attacks, but it will be renovated from a house to a stronghold that can send out one arrow after the next, against his defenses.

So let's make this practical. What is your weakness? Where does the enemy attack you the most? Which circumstance, words, or thoughts tend to bring the flesh out of you?

KEY PRINCIPLE

> When the promises and reality of the Word is more of a reality to you than what is around about you – you just put the blueprint together for a stronghold, in Christ.

Ok, you have a place to start. Now what I want you to do is to go through the Word and pull out scriptures that are arrows against each of these attacks. If you are not sure where to start looking, I have included a list of powerful promises that you can use according to your need. They should be enough to give you a good kick-start.

Now that you have your promise in hand, read it through. Now stop and visualize it! See it, smell it, taste it and feel it! So let us take my example of fear of financial lack. Here is a good passage that I can build my faith on:

> *Psalms 45:12 And the daughter of Tyre will come with a gift; the rich among the people will seek your favor.*

I can see the merchant ships coming to me on the ocean. I can feel ocean spray on my face and taste the saltiness on my skin. The smell of the seas wafts over me as I see the rich leave the ship – each laying a treasure at my feet. They are clothes in these brightly colored clothes from all over the world. Each one is entreating my favor.

I rule and I reign in Christ! Come on now, you are a prophet, I know that you have a powerful imagination! Add some life to the Word. Live in it. Breath in it. Allow its pictures to shape the way you think.

As I applied these principles in my own life, the enemy was foolish enough to try his tricks again. We hit a sudden slump and all our accounts were drained with a huge list of bills due the next day. In the past, I would have been crushed.

I looked around me and I laughed. I did not see the empty balances. I saw those princes. I saw the storehouse of the Lord pouring out over me. In that moment I felt His presence around me and as I smiled and reached up to take hold of His hand the yoke of the enemy was broken.

I did not need to fight. I did not have to bind any demon. I just had to stand in the truth. The truth was that God had provided my needs according to His riches in glory. The truth was that God had never let me down. The truth was that the inheritance was mine.

I was not moved – satan was moved. From there, things began to snowball in ways I could never have imagined.

EMOTIONS

A deep peace came over me and my mustard seed of faith began leaping inside of me! It felt as if it was just waiting for the opportunity to be let loose. My faith had been a sheathed sword!

All my fear and sinful reactions were a heavy leather sheath that had my sword strapped to my side. I knew it was there. I knew God's Word was true, but I felt impotent in my ability to fight back.

When I allowed the pictures of my mind to come in line with the Word of God, the hindrances were removed and I looked down to see that broad sword firmly placed in the palm of my hand.

Now that felt good. There is no feeling quite like realizing that you have control over the winds and the waves in your life. The knowledge gave rise to a thunderous rise up emotion from deep within. What did I feel? A blend of anger, righteousness, excitement and outright conviction.

It struck me. "I do not have to take this. God has answered before I asked. My God is all powerful!"

Emotion born out of the reality of the Word empowers you to take the land. It is not a struggle! Prophet of God… warfare is not and should not ever, be a struggle.

> **KEY PRINCIPLE**
>
> Spiritual warfare should be a rush of emotion based on what you know, released through faith.

This is not what happened in the past though is it? Circumstances surrounded you like a hungry wolf, and fear was born. That emotion also gave rise to action, but it was motivated by a spirit from the enemy.

Is it no wonder that everything you set your hand to, fell at your feet? If you try to take action based on an emotion born out of the flesh, you are fighting in the wrong camp!

WILL

Fear gives birth to fear. An action made on the basis of fear is a force giving the enemy more license in your life. Do not get mad at the Lord if what you set your hand to keeps failing.

When you set your hand to the task, did you do so through a conviction from the Holy Spirit? What birthed your action? Whatever birthed your action owns it. I pray then that it was born through the agency of the Holy Spirit, and a conviction in the Word of God!

We often misunderstand this simple principle. The enemy comes in like a lion and instead of just standing and not allowing ourselves to be moved, we run in a hundred directions all at once. You try to fight the enemy with the flesh.

You try to overcome the circumstance in the flesh. Is it any wonder then that you end up tying yourself up in knots? The worst part of this all, is that this leads to another bad experience, and so reinforces the deep rooted scars of bad experiences that you already have had in your life.

The temptation in these moments, is to get angry at the Lord for letting you down. Did the Lord let you down? Did he tell you to take action? Did he tell you to run off in a hundred directions to try and "make things right"?

If not, then why are you getting angry because He did not bless the work of your hands? You want God to bless the work of your hands? Why don't you ask Him where to work first?

You cannot do things the devil's way and then ask God to bless it. That is like saying, "I am going to fight for the enemy for a minute. Lord could you strengthen my arm?

Time To Do Things God's Way

So we are back to our main point here. If you want to overcome every work of the enemy, you need to do things God's way. There is only one way to do that – your actions have to be based on the reality of the Word.

Once your mind is conditioned by the truth of the Word, instead of the deception of your circumstances, your emotions begin to build up all the power you need to begin taking your land back.

Your action adds the fuel and trigger to your weapon of warfare. All that is left now… is to give the command.

The angels are standing by. The Holy Spirit is standing by. Can you hear the clink of armor as each soldier shifts on their feet?

There is a slight intake of breath and a momentary lapse in silence as they wait for the command. Armor has been polished until it shines like lightening. You feel the hilt of your sword has been formed perfectly to every curve of your hand.

It is as if the whole world waits for the word. They wait to hear the battle cry. A cry that has been used since the day of creation and is used even today, by the saints of God.

The silence is broken. The word has gone forth. Not in fear, not in pain and not in the flesh. It has gone forth in faith. With a mighty rushing wind, the Holy Spirit mounts the wind and sweeps across the land. The angels follow hard at His heels, engaging in warfare at the highest level.

Your word of faith is a chain reaction in the spirit realm. Train and become equipped. Own it. The Church depends on it.

CHAPTER 12

ARM YOURSELF

CHAPTER 12 – ARM YOURSELF

No one goes into battle unarmed. That is the lesson I learned when feeding my five month old for the first time. As things turned out, he was not terribly fond of cereal. It was easy to tell as well, because when I put something into his mouth he did not like the taste of – he responded by spraying it right on back to me.

It did not take long for me to realize that to win this war I had to clothe myself and drape all surrounding furniture. Whether the battle you are facing today is as simple as trying to convince a baby that there is nothing tastier than smashed peas or you are taking on the hordes of hell – for your safety, you need to arm yourself!

> *Ephesians 6:13 Therefore take up the whole armor of God, that you may be able to withstand in the evil day, and having done all, to stand.*
> *14 Stand therefore, having girded your waist with truth, having put on the breastplate of righteousness,*
> *15 and having shod your feet with the preparation of the gospel of peace;*
> *16 above all, taking the shield of faith with which you will be able to quench all the fiery darts of the wicked one.*
> *17 And take the helmet of salvation, and the sword of the Spirit, which is the word of God:*

You have to go prepared for every eventuality. It is the same for spiritual warfare. You cannot go in and say, "Let's just see how it goes and go with the flow."

We have already covered the fact that you do not wrestle with flesh and blood, but with principalities and powers. Now that the point is well drilled home, it is time to get ready! Just after Paul points us to the heavenly battlegrounds, he tells us just what we need to be armed with. So how do you arm yourself to battle in the heavenlies?

I am going to go through each bit of the armor, step by step. As I share this, I want you to make a note because each part builds on the next.

Gird Your Loins

Number one, gird your loins with truth. Truth is probably the most powerful weapon of all, because when you know the truth, it sets you free. Sometimes, that is half the warfare over with.

As we have been studying about knowing your enemy and understanding warfare, your first reality is that you do not need to take these attacks. You do not need to settle for curses in your life. Most importantly, you can overcome.

There is no use putting on the rest of the armor, if you haven't even put on truth yet. Until you know that you can overcome and you realize that you do not have to take these attacks, you have not even begun.

If you are hoping that your conviction will be found along the way, then you are just doing warfare for the sake of doing warfare.

"Let's go into warfare today."

"I bind you, Lucifer. I bind you, Pharaoh. I bind you, Apollyon."

What are you doing this for?

Name Your Cause

Any great battle in history was driven by purpose. There was land that needed to be taken back. There was a cause. What is your cause today?

I think some prophets just like warfare because they can blame everything on the devil. However, unless you know that you can overcome this enemy, you are just doing warfare with strong hope and no faith at all.

So, are your loins girded with truth today? Are they strapped securely to you with the aid of strong conviction?

> **Key Principle**
>
> Gird your loins with truth. Truth is probably the most powerful weapon of all, because when you know the truth, it sets you free.

Most importantly, when you look at the condition of your spirit right now, are you saying, "I have the power to overcome through Jesus Christ? I do not have to take this! I can overcome?"

Once you get this initial conviction, then you are ready to step up and put on the breastplate of righteousness.

BREASTPLATE OF RIGHTEOUSNESS

Loins girded? Good. Now we can fit your breastplate. What does the breastplate of righteousness talk about? It simply means to be in right standing with God.

2 Corinthians 5:21 says,

> *For He made Him who knew no sin to be sin for us, that we might become the righteousness of God in Him.*

You are righteous because of the blood. You can go into this warfare, not because you are really good at it, but because of the power of His blood.

Fitting your breastplate securely over your heart you should be saying, "Lord, I stand before you in all my weakness. I lay my sin on the cross and stand in you – not in my works."

If there is anything in your life that is giving satan any license, now is a good time to deal with it. Trying to go into battle when satan has license in your life is like taking on the enemy without a breastplate. Sure, you might give him a good smack or two, but is that heart of yours hidden safely under the blood of righteousness?

Yes, you do not have to take these attacks or curses. Yes, you have the power to overcome. However, you also had the power to give the enemy license in the first place remember?

When you come under His blood, you realize that you have the victory in Christ.

Yes, the truth is that you do not have to take any attack from satan and you are the overcomer, but you need to come into right standing with God first.

You cannot just go running at the enemy without getting armed first. One of the most important parts of arming yourself is realizing that His blood cleanses you.

If there is any guilt in your heart right now, if there is any doubt, fear, or anger that is preventing you from coming to the throne room of God with boldness - this is where you stop and deal with it. Take a moment to submit before you start shouting your mouth off at the enemy.

It does not take long to put on the breastplate of righteousness and come into right standing with God. He already died for your sins. All you have to do is confess and get your heart right. Then, watch out devil, because nothing can stop you now.

The Gospel of Peace

I know how much we love the drama, but the truth is that the greatest victory comes when there is a profound absence of anxiety in your heart.

You need peace in your spirit. That is why you have to do the "breastplate part" first. You can only come to this place of peace when you have dealt with the sin in your life.

If you are dwelling on your sin or the hard circumstances you are facing, there is a temptation to feel angry or overwhelmed. If you are running the gauntlet panicking as you yell, "I am so angry at the devil! The blood, the blood, the blood!" Then you are not acting in faith. Jesus did not need to shout at the devil on Calvary to take him out. Although the truth be told, it does certainly feel good to give him a piece of your mind. Regardless, do so in peace and allow the anger rising up from deep inside to be righteous and not fleshly.

When you are reacting in the flesh, you are not exactly carrying out the gospel of peace in that moment. You are just having a hissy fit. Calm down. The devil is going to ignore you.

Learn "The Tone"

Sometimes, I have one of those "mommy days". Days when the kids have not done their chores and I walk into a bedroom that looks like a bomb hit it. Then, I walk into my bathroom and they have used up all my toiletries again.

All it is going to take for me to fall off the edge is to walk into my kitchen, to find my favorite (an expensive) carving knife being used to cut plastic.

That is just about enough! I suddenly have a hysterical moment. I spit and spew, jumping up and down. Four little faces stare back at me wide-eyed. I can read their minds.

"There goes mom. She is at it again. She will calm down any second now and everything will be ok." The worst part? They are right! I am just freaking out.

Then there are times when I walk into the lounge and see that my son tried to sneak a video game during his schooling hours. All I need to do is give them "the look". Then I say, "You will turn that off and find your way to your desk right now. You do that again and I am banning you from playing for the rest of the month."

I do not need to raise my voice or get hysterical. I barely even need to talk. He jumps up and does it because he knows, "Do not mess with mom right now. She has 'the tone' and she means what she says."

The enemy knows "the tone" too. He knows when you are having a hissy fit - binding and loosing just because you are having a bad day.

You think that the louder you get, the more it makes satan tremble.

"I bind you satan!" Nothing happens.

"I BIND YOU SATAN!" Still nothing.

"**I BIND YOU SATAN!**" Nope... you are not getting it.

Just because you know how to use the full extent of your vocal cords does not mean that satan will now be bound and tremble before you.

Where is your authority and peace? The greatest authority comes out of rest - not out of hysteria. When you are convinced of a principle and stand in faith, you are at rest.

You see, satan knows you are covered by the blood. He knows your position in Christ. He probably knows it better than you do.

Question is... do you know it?

Are you settled enough in your peace? I have a little line that I like, "Don't react... Act."

Don't React... Act

Don't react to your circumstances, don't react to the enemy, and don't react to the curses.

Don't react to anything that is going on. Act in peace because that is where the power is. If you have to stand up and scream and shout at the devil until you are hoarse, you do not have any authority.

You should be able to look at him in the eye and say, "Get out of here… NOW!" When he hears that, he should be running his legs off because he knows that you know who you have at your back.

So, firstly, get your conviction that is found in girding your loins in truth. Then buckle up with right standing before God. Once these two pieces of armor are on place, you are already feeling pretty good at yourself. In fact, you are looking downright terrifying as the emblem of the Holy Spirit gleams from your breastplate.

Let me tell you, there is nothing more terrifying than a well-trained warrior who does not flinch in the face of the enemy. The comical foot soldier jumping up and down make you laugh at their antics, does not give off an air of authority.

> **KEY PRINCIPLE**
>
> The greatest authority comes out of rest - not out of hysteria. When you are convinced of a principle and stand in faith, you are at rest.

The one to be feared is the bulky, well-armed brute of a man that does not blink in the face of danger.

Just looking at him you know that something unexpected is about to burst out of him. Keep the devil guessing. Stand in peace. Once you have stared him down without blinking, you are ready to pick up your shield.

Shield of Faith

What is the shield of faith? It is to know that you know. This follows on so beautifully from the gospel of peace.

When you come into rest, the noise stops round about you.

Yes, you are in the middle of warfare. Circumstances are rebelling against you and the voices of others are flying over your head as poison tipped arrows.

Your body is under attack, your finances are being tested and everything you tried to do failed. When you come to rest in the middle of that, an eerie silence hangs in the air. In this moment a deep conviction begins to build up from deep within.

Without making any fuss, you pick up your shield of faith and you believe His word.

In times past you might have been rattled, but today is a new day. You have been trained in boot camp. You have found your conviction upon the cross. You have endured weapon's training and learned how to use what God has given to you. It has shaped your mind, emotions and will.

The man that was, is no more. Instead of a victim, the enemy turns to see a warrior standing before him. This prophet of God, is what it looks like!

With each nail you received on the cross. With each battle maneuver you had to learn, you were establishing your shield of faith. Each time you submitted your sin to Him and allowed Him to change you, He was etching His crest on your shield.

You will only pick up the fullness of it as the battle is arrayed against you. It is only when you have a conviction, are upon the cross and come to peace that you know… that you know… that you know, that you are the overcomer.

The storm is silenced before you. The winds and waves cease. Now you understand. Now you know! Now you stand.

Helmet of Salvation

It is now time to set God's people free. Standing in faith will allow your eyes to see something you never did before. The true Gospel of Christ. A Gospel that says,

"We are saved from poverty and sickness."

"You can expect victory, provision, and peace."

"You can expect things to change."

You put on a possibility mentality and turn around to survey the land. You see the Church stuck in a rut. You see believers struggling under the heavy load placed on their shoulders.

You see spiritual babies questioning their salvation. You see the small lambs being tossed aside or getting lost. Your spiritual eyes are opened and the battlefield reveals the broken and cast down. You see those that the Lord has called you to pick up.

To put on the helmet of salvation is to have the mind of Christ. It means to see as He sees. To feel as He feels. It is only when you put on the helmet of salvation that you are equipped to reach down and pick up those that are crying out to Him for deliverance.

The moment those visions and revelations begin to bubble up from deep within, your heart will beat fast in the breastplate of righteousness. You will be reminded of the truth of the Word. Do not engage in spiritual warfare without this revelation.

Until you see as Christ sees, you are entering into this battlefield as a blind man. You can be equipped from head to toe, but if you are blind, you will not see the enemy behind you. You will trip over the wounded and end up fighting on the wrong side.

Once you know your place in Christ, it is time for your eyes to be opened to the spiritual realm. It is time to have the helmet of salvation. In this moment it will not take much for your hand to reach for your sword.

The Sword of the Spirit

It is time to take this land. I only need to see a precious lamb broken and bleeding by the wayside to want to take out the devouring lion standing over it. Nothing in this world can hold me back. The anger is no longer mine. This offense against me is made personal the moment I see satan using his ploys to destroy a precious child of God.

I take it personally when I see him leading people astray through heresy. I take it personally when I see marriages being torn apart and children being abused. I get angry when I see a church being made fun of and blinded to the real ploys of satan.

Your sword is the most offensive weapon that you have. The rest are all defensive weapons. Up until now we have covered you with the blood and opened your spiritual eyes.

Now the question remains – now that you can "see" what will you do about it? That is where the sword comes into play.

Realize that this is not your idea. This is God's idea. This is where you stand and say, "Satan, you bow. Mountain, you be removed. Circumstances, you come right. Apollyon, get out of here.

I bind you, spirits of infirmity. I close those doors. I loose that blessing. I bind that thing. I plant that thing. I uproot that thing."

You do whatever is necessary, but you cannot do that if you have not first armed yourself. If you pick up your sword without the rest of your armor – you are powerless.

Here is where I see a downfall amongst many prophets. They go from the first to the last step and leave out all the pieces in-between.

Then, they cannot understand why there is no power. Picking up your sword is the easiest part actually. You know very well how to bind and loose. You have been doing that ever since you got a conviction of your call.

Prophets are great at that. They can intercede, pray, and bring heaven down to earth. They are mighty warriors that know how to wield a sword, but what about the pieces in between that give the sword a target?

Are you just full of hot air? Are you slashing your sword wildly in the air or do you have intent and purpose? Are you going to cut where it counts? Are you going to break the enemy where he can be broken or are you just flapping your lips and sounding off?

Let's get result to your prayers. Let us see real results when you do spiritual warfare.

LET'S RECAP

1. Do You Know the Truth?

2. Have you dealt with your sin, your guilt, and your fears?
3. Have you come to peace or are you running around being hysterical?
4. Are you holding your shield of faith?
5. Is your warfare stemming from revelation and direction from the Spirit?
6. Finally, are you taking your faith, conviction and authority and sending words of power into the earth?

When you have all of those other things behind you, you just need to point that sword in the right direction and it will hit its mark every time.

Now its time to praise the Lord for the victory. Proclaim the victory.

"Thank you Lord that I have the victory. I have overcome. You have overcome the world, so we have overcome it too."

Prophet, remember this, it is necessary to do warfare, but no one lives on the battlefield.

You cannot live there, but make sure that your time standing in blood and dust is effective. Your victory does not need to be a travail. When you have the upper hand, this is not a battle that will last for long.

THE AVERAGE DURATION OF A BATTLE

How long does it take me to tell the enemy to get packing? Five minutes? What takes the time is getting into His righteousness and getting into the Word. The longer part of your equipping is coming to the point where you speak with the anointing, expecting results.

So how long does it take to tell the enemy to run?

"Get lost."

There - I just did it in two words. It does not take a lot of time. You do not have to spend an hour in tongues, interpretation, and warfare, binding every demon in Hell.

If I have to tell my son to do the same thing twice, then either he did not hear me or I am really not standing in my authority.

Dump the idea that warfare needs to be so intense. No, the devil should listen the first time. Otherwise, you are not speaking clearly enough or you do not have any faith and he knows it.

Warfare is the quick part. So, get on with it. Get your spirit in place. Engage in warfare, and then get into praise and thank the Lord for the victory. Then, continue as though the battle is already won.

> **KEY PRINCIPLE**
>
> Dump the idea that warfare needs to be so intense. The devil should listen the first time.

That is faith, is it not? Faith is past tense. The battle has been won. That is the best conviction of all.

Jesus won the battle for you two thousand years ago. Satan has not suddenly been loosed on the earth so that you have to single-handedly bring him back down to Hell.

PUTTING ON CHRIST

It is for you to come to that conviction and that is what I have been leading you to. That is what putting on the armor is all about. It is about putting on Christ.

That is why the Scriptures say, "Once you have done all, stand." Once you have put on the whole armor of God, you stand.

Do not think for a moment that the fun is now over. For you, prophet of God, it has just begun. You have subdued the enemy and put him in place. Now your work can really begin.

What is, after all, the greatest battle strategy of all? It is to be on the offence! There is no greater offence that establishing the will of God. There is only one surefire way to not only win back your land, but to maintain it. That way is by realizing that once all is said and done, you do not stand alone.

You are not empowered just to bind demons and you are not anointed for the entertainment of it. Once you are done tearing down, it is time to begin building up and establishing God's plan. Follow me closely as I lead you to what lies beyond the battlefield.

CHAPTER 13

ANGELS AT ARMS

Chapter 13 – Angels at Arms

> *Revelation 12:7 And war broke out in heaven: Michael and his angels fought with the dragon; and the dragon and his angels fought,*
> *8 but they did not prevail, nor was a place found for them in heaven any longer.*

We are the Goliath on this battlefield, and the sooner you see that, the sooner you will look up and see that you do not fight alone. When you look at the structure of how satan works, you can often forget that he is not the only one who has helpers.

Consider that just a third of the angels fell with satan. Let's do the math here. This means that they are outnumbered two to one! It is no wonder that just one of us can send a thousand demons to flight, and two, ten thousand!

So what is the catch? What are the angels waiting for? Well that is simple – they are waiting to hear the Word of God. It is faith that moves the angels to action and without it, they will stand around waiting for it.

We have looked at the covenant that God entered into with man, and the authority he gave Adam when He created the earth. Here is the reality – the Lord handed the dominion over the earth to us. If we want to see change on earth as it is in heaven, it means giving the Lord license.

Consider it like this. The King gives a decree and so the generals and officers take up that decree and lead the troops to war. Although the King might fight by their side, he does not win the war alone.

Yet how many times have you stood back and waited for God to do the job? Here is a truth prophet of God – God has given you the authority to subdue this earth. He is waiting for you to use what He has given to you. He is waiting for you to come to the Throne Room, get the decree, and then to use it as a sword in the earth so that His work can be done. This is what it looks like.

THE OMEGA OF SPIRITUAL WARFARE

> *Isaiah 55:10 For as the rain comes down, and the snow from heaven, and do not return there, but water the earth, and make it bring forth and bud, that it may give seed to the sower and bread to the eater,*
> *11 So shall My word be that goes forth from My mouth; It shall not return to Me void, but it shall accomplish what I please, and it shall prosper in the thing for which I sent it.*

What is it that releases a creative force in this earth? Well according to Isaiah, it is the Word of God that creates. So tell me prophet, how will God speak forth that word?

It is through the mouth of man! A man containing the spirit of God, made up of the elements of this earth. When such a man speaks forth the ordained word of

God under His direction and anointing, it is released as a creative force.

This is the omega of spiritual warfare. The final word – the definitive standard. With just a breath of His mouth, the Lord divided the Red Sea, however Moses had to raise his staff first.

The water flowed from the rock, but Moses had to speak it forth first. Sure, the walls of Jericho came down, but to cause the foundations of Jericho to shake, the people had to shout!

You can have all the principles and understand just how satan is getting in, but until you send forth the word of God with faith and authority, warfare has not even begun.

Giving God License

The enemy gains his license to attack through the sin of man. Yes, you can patch up those walls and take that license away. It will most certainly make your walk a lot easier. Yet I tell you that there is an even better way.

What if you just gave the Lord license instead of the enemy? You know that satan uses his license to attack our souls, circumstances, and through the systems around us. His attacks make it difficult to make the right choices.

Sure, you still have a choice. Regardless of what happens to you in this world, you can still choose whether to do things righteously or in sin. Sometimes though it is difficult. The attacks come upon you like waves to the point where you feel your emotions cave to what you see around you.

After one wave after another of physical, emotional, and spiritual attack, you feel your arms beginning to drop. You are like Moses on top of the mountain. He knows keeping his arms raised gives God the upper hand, but he still is overcome with weariness.

> **KEY PRINCIPLE**
>
> Instead of giving the enemy license through sin, how about giving the Lord license in your life and circumstances instead?

However, what if the influences coming upon you created an environment for blessing? In other words, what if the thoughts and feelings coming your way made making the righteous decision easy?

Instead of being attacked with fear and guilt, you wake up overcome with joy and peace? Well that is exactly what this passage is talking about right here!

> *Galatians 5:22 But the fruit of the Spirit is love, joy, peace, longsuffering, kindness, goodness, faithfulness,*
> *23 gentleness, self- control. Against such there*

> *is no law.*
> *24 And those who are Christ's have crucified the flesh with its passions and desires.*

Imagine walking along when you are suddenly overwhelmed with love, patience, gentleness, and self control!

Is it a myth? Don't you understand the price Jesus paid for you yet? He paid the price not just for your redemption, but also to save you! He died to save you from the work of the evil one – to remove from you the influences of this world that make serving God so difficult.

He died so that you could overcome and not just beat up the devil, but give God enough license in your life to walk in blessing every day of your life.

The way of the cross is a lot more than just going to heaven one day. It is about learning to bring heaven down to the earth. So let's get practical here. How do we make this a reality?

How do we bring heaven to earth as prophets? How can you surround yourself and your future generations with a continual righteous influence?

You are well aware of those generational curses! The influences surround you with thoughts and voices seducing you to sin. The spirit of lust whispers in your ear and distracts you with the smell of perfume.

Anger and bitterness lure you into their arms with words of comfort and promise. Promises that turn sour in your stomach and turn your life into a wasteland.

Each time you surrender, you give satan a stronghold in your life. The worst of it, is that influence is then passed down to future generations. How about you start a new generational influence today?

What if you were surrounded with the words of God, and the sudden desire to walk in holiness? What if you did not have to fight off the seductive voice of temptation, but could hear, quite clearly, the voice of the Spirit? You have in your spirit the ability to make this a reality. Not only that, but once you make it a reality in your life, you will naturally pass it on to your generations.

Your children will grow up with the gentle voice of Jesus being their influence instead of the seduction of satan! Prophet of God, can't you see the incredible inheritance that the Lord has called you to birth into this earth? Starting from your generation and spreading throughout the members of the Body – you can bear an influence that will empower us against every work of the enemy.

That leaves the big question, doesn't it? How? It's simple – instead of giving satan the run of each battlefield – you give it to the Lord instead!

The Battlefield of the Mind

> *Psalms 77:11 I will remember the works of the Lord; surely I will remember Your wonders of old.*
> *12 I will also meditate on all Your work, and talk of Your deeds.*

I have already taught you the power of the Word and how to use it to change your mind. By renewing your mind, it conditions you to make the correct choices. When all that has been fed into your mind is defeat and strife, this will always be your response to every problem you face.

Each time the enemy attacks, you will react with bitterness and frustration. However, when you dwell so much on the promises that God has given to you, those promises begin to become your reality. They predispose you to the blessing of God.

When we were facing a lot of attack and I was struggling with the fears in my mind, the Lord gave me a fantastic project that I want to give you to do today. He told me to bring to remembrance every single promise that He had given to me.

God's Promises

So I went through my journals and I wrote each one of them down. Once I had done that, the Lord told me to visualize each one. To live in it until it became a reality.

He told me to dwell on them every single time fear or doubt came into my heart. Bit by bit the fear was displaced with faith. The disappointment was displaced with hope!

Whatever you are focusing on, will form the pictures in your mind. What are you focusing on today? The devil? Your problems? When you focus on the promises of God, they become your reality. Once that happens faith is born.

Once I had my neat little list of promises, the Lord had me do something else that solidified them. He told me to bring to memory any clear instructions that He had given me along with them. You will realize that with any promises that the Lord has given to you, He also gave you a direction or a commandment.

He had me ask myself, "Have I been obedient to do what the Lord said?"

The Lord told Abraham that He was going to be a father of nations, but that he first had to leave everyone and everything he knew behind.

OBEDIENCE

Would the children of Israel have ever possessed the Promised Land if Abraham had not been obedient to God, leaving his heritage behind?

It is the same with you. You want the promises of God to come to pass, but are you prepared to be obedient to see them manifest in your life?

So along with that list of promises, ask yourself, "Have I been obedient?" How can you expect the Lord to give you the word of decree to bring about the promise, if you were not obedient enough to open your mouth?

God promised Joshua the city of Jericho, but there were a few steps he had to take first! The Lord promised David the crown, but he had to fight for it. Yes, the Lord will open the doors, but until you walk through them in the manner He dictates, how will His creative word have any place to germinate in your life?

THE BATTLEFIELD OF CIRCUMSTANCES

Once I had come to the place of meditating on His promises until I could see, touch, and taste them, the Lord took me a step further. He told me to look at my circumstances and compare them to the things that He had promised me.

When I looked around at my life and ministry, I realized that there were a lot of things that were not in line. I am not sure what I was waiting for. I guess I was waiting for God to "just do it." He gave the promise and so He would "just do it."

However, I needed a bit more than that! That promise had to be released into the earth through faith! So the Lord told me to clearly identify circumstances that were not in line with His will.

Much like he told Joshua that everywhere he placed his feet was his, He had me take a spiritual walk! A walk to call forth my circumstances into line. To give the Lord license in my life and to call those things that were not, as though they were.

No wonder He had me meditate on His promises until I believed them with all my heart.

If I had try to tackle my circumstances before I had faith, I would have sent forth words of desperate hope and good intention – not words of faith!

Change did not happen overnight. The enemy had been slinging circumstances at me for so long that I had simply accepted them. However, when I began to compare God's promises with what I saw in my life, a new conviction rose up inside of me.

I no longer accepted what I saw. It was time to own this battlefield! The Lord had me take back my land daily! I stood daily on His Word and the promises He had given to me in the spirit, and He had me call my circumstances into obedience!

As if my circumstances were a disobedient child that had gone astray, I grabbed them by the scruff of their neck and brought them into submission!

Many times when I prayed, I saw my circumstances as a road that had become crooked and narrow, making it hard for God's promises to come to me. I called those paths straight and broad!

> **KEY PRINCIPLE**
>
> Circumstances that are in rebellion to the promises of God are mountains that need to be uprooted.

Bit by bit circumstances began to change until they obeyed the word of God. What do you think God meant when He said to cast a mountain into the sea?

Who goes around just casting mountains into the sea? What did the poor mountain ever do to you? However, what if the enemy has planted a mountain in your path. Do you try to climb it or go around it? No way! It is time to uproot it!

Circumstances that are in rebellion to the promises of God are mountains that need to be uprooted. Don't just stand there, prophet of God, take the faith in your belly, the sword in your hand, and the Word in your mouth, and call forth those changes!

THE BATTLEFIELD OF SYSTEMS

You do not need to look far to see that satan's favorite battlefield is the systems of the world – and why not? He has spent thousands of years setting them neatly into place.

Now you could try and tackle those systems, or you could just switch up the game. Give Jesus dominion of them instead. You could try to tear down governments... or just put Jesus on the throne.

You could try to dismember the financial system – or just hand the reins over to the Lord so that the Church finds favor.

Isn't that what this passage means?

> *Job 27:16 Though he heaps up silver like dust, and piles up clothing like clay -*
> *17 He may pile it up, but the just will wear it, and the innocent will divide the silver.*

How exactly did you imagine all that silver and clothing was to suddenly appear in the hands of the just? It is simple, just give the Lord dominion over it and I promise – He will be more than happy to distribute it accordingly!

So often we feel we have to fight in this world, when all we need is favor. We just need someone on our side in high places. Well you do not get any higher than the King of Kings. When you give him license and put Him on the throne, the rest is simple.

This is the main battlefield of the prophet! This is what Jeremiah understood when the Lord told him that he would build up and tear down – to root up and to plant! That is what you learned in the study on intercession and decree in the *Prophetic Anointing* book. Remember what you gained there?

Well now it is time to use it at a new level. It is time to apply it to this level of warfare that does a whole lot more than bind satan. This warfare gives the Lord control over matters in the earth.

It means praying, "I call these systems into line in the name of Jesus! Holy Spirit I put you in control! I call the financial and political systems into obedience!"

It means applying 2 Corinthians 10 and bearing spiritual pressure on every high place and every system to come under subjection!

Isn't this what God told Adam to do? He told Adam to subdue the earth. That commandment has not changed and now with the indwelling of the Holy Spirit, and empowered by the anointing, we have what we need to do just that.

The Lord Jesus Christ is our King and ruler over the Kingdom in which we serve. He is a King that has chosen to share His throne with us. A throne whose place it is to rule and reign in this earth.

He gained the rights to rule the systems of this world. The enemy and his demons have stirred up the hearts of man to sin and give them the license to oust the Lord. It will not take much for you to stand strong and to claim back what he has tried to steal.

All you need is a conviction and the authority. The Word of God will give you the conviction as well as the authority. All that is left for you to do is to use it.

There is no better passage that concludes this book than the one below:

> *2 Corinthians 10:3 For though we walk in the flesh, we do not war according to the flesh. 4 For the weapons of our warfare are not carnal but mighty in God for pulling down strongholds, 5 casting down arguments and every high thing that exalts itself against the knowledge of God, bringing every thought into captivity to the obedience of Christ;*

Although we might have failures and sin, we do not need to fight back with natural strengths. We do not need to battle all on our own, feeling weak and unarmed. We do not war after the flesh. We do not war with man. We do not war with our neighbors.

We war with the kingdom of darkness that seeks to dethrone the Lord in this earth. The reality is that although you and I are living a chapter in this book, the ending has already been written. It says in the book of Revelation that although the dragon and his demons came against the Archangel Michael and his angels, they were defeated!

Satan was defeated when he tried to take God's throne. He was cast into the pit of hell. He was defeated on Calvary when he crucified Christ. He remains defeated today, and all you and I need to do, is to keep watch and maintain the land that belongs to us.

It is for us to cast down the imaginations of our heart and mind that lead us astray. It is for us to identify where satan is getting his license. Above all, it is up to us to keep God on the throne and to allow Him to speak forth the word through us that will continue to bring His plan to pass.

Those are your marching orders prophetic warrior. You have been armed. You have been trained. You have been given directions. Now go out, taking all you have gained, and set God's people free.

BONUS CHAPTER

SCRIPTURE PROMISES

BONUS MATERIALS – SCRIPTURE PROMISES

As promised in Chapter 11, below are a list of promises from the Word to meditate on to renew your mind.

HEALING

Deuteronomy 7:15
And the Lord will take away from you all sickness, and will afflict you with none of the terrible diseases of Egypt which you have known, but will lay them on all those who hate you.

Exodus 23:25
So you shall serve the Lord your God, and He will bless your bread and your water. And I will take sickness away from the midst of you.

Exodus 23:26
No one shall suffer miscarriage or be barren in your land; I will fulfill the number of your days.

Galatians 3:13
Christ has redeemed us from the curse of the law, having become a curse for us (for it is written, "Cursed is everyone who hangs on a tree").

Isaiah 40:31
But those who wait on the Lord shall renew their strength; they shall mount up with wings like eagles, they shall run and not be weary, they shall walk and not faint.

John 15:7
If you abide in Me, and My words abide in you, you will ask what you desire, and it shall be done for you.

PROVISION

2 Chronicles 15:7
But you, be strong and do not let your hands be weak, for your work shall be rewarded.

Deuteronomy 28:2
And all these blessings shall come upon you and overtake you, because you obey the voice of the Lord your God.

Deuteronomy 28:8
he Lord will command the blessing on you in your storehouses and in all to which you set your hand, and He will bless you in the land which the Lord your God is giving you.

Ephesians 3:20
Now to Him who is able to do exceedingly abundantly above all that we ask or think, according to the power that works in us,

Esther 5:6
What is your petition? It shall be granted you. What is your request, up to half the kingdom? It shall be done.

John 10:10
The thief does not come except to steal, and to kill, and to destroy. I have come that they may have life, and that they may have it more abundantly.

VICTORY

2 Chronicles 16:9
For the eyes of the Lord run to and fro throughout the whole earth, to show Himself strong on behalf of those whose heart is loyal to Him. In this you have done foolishly; therefore from now on you shall have wars.

2 Chronicles 20:17
You will not need to fight in this battle. Position yourselves, stand still and see the salvation of the Lord, who is with you, O Judah and Jerusalem!' Do not fear or be dismayed; tomorrow go out against them, for the Lord is with you.

2 Corinthians 10:4
For the weapons of our warfare are not carnal but mighty in God for pulling down strongholds.

Deuteronomy 3:22
You must not fear them, for the Lord your God Himself fights for you.

Deuteronomy 11:25
No man shall be able to stand against you; the

Lord your God will put the dread of you and the fear of you upon all the land where you tread, just as He has said to you.

1 John 4:4
You are of God, little children, and have overcome them, because He who is in you is greater than he who is in the world.

ASSURANCE

1 Corinthians 1:30
But of Him you are in Christ Jesus, who became for us wisdom from God—and righteousness and sanctification and redemption—.

1 Corinthians 10:13
No temptation has overtaken you except such as is common to man; but God is faithful, who will not allow you to be tempted beyond what you are able, but with the temptation will also make the way of escape, that you may be able to bear it.

Deuteronomy 31:6
Be strong and of good courage, do not fear nor be afraid of them; for the Lord your God, He is the One who goes with you. He will not leave you nor forsake you.

Galatians 4:7
Therefore you are no longer a slave but a son, and if a son, then an heir of God through Christ.

Hebrews 7:25
Therefore He is also able to save to the uttermost those who come to God through Him, since He always lives to make intercession for them.

Romans 8:28
And we know that all things work together for good to those who love God, to those who are the called according to His purpose.

GENERAL

1 Corinthians 2:12
Now we have received, not the spirit of the world, but the Spirit who is from God, that we might know the things that have been freely given to us by God.

Daniel 4:3
How great are His signs, and how mighty His wonders! His kingdom is an everlasting kingdom, and His dominion is from generation to generation.

Deuteronomy 7:9
Therefore know that the Lord your God, He is God, the faithful God who keeps covenant and mercy for a thousand generations with those who love Him and keep His commandments.

Deuteronomy 28:3
Blessed shall you be in the city, and blessed shall you be in the country.

Ephesians 3:20
Now to Him who is able to do exceedingly abundantly above all that we ask or think, according to the power that works in us.

Hebrews 4:16
Let us therefore come boldly to the throne of grace, that we may obtain mercy and find grace to help in time of need.

These are just to get you started. We encourage you to find your own promises in the word.

About the Author

Born in Bulawayo, Zimbabwe and raised in South Africa, Colette had a zeal to serve the Lord from a young age. Coming from a long line of Christian leaders and having grown up as a pastor's kid she is no stranger to the realities of ministry. Despite having to endure many hardships such as her parent's divorce, rejection, and poverty, she continues to follow after the Lord passionately. Overcoming these obstacles early in her life has built a foundation of compassion and desire to help others gain victory in their lives.

Since then, the Lord has led Colette, with her husband Craig Toach, to establish *Apostolic Movement International,* a ministry to train and minister to Christian leaders all over the world, where they share all the wisdom that the Lord has given them through each and every time they chose to walk through the refining fire in their personal lives, as well as in ministry.

In addition, Colette is a fantastic cook, an amazing mom to not only her 4 natural children, but to her numerous spiritual children all over the world. Colette is also a renowned author, mentor, trainer and a woman that has great taste in shoes! The scripture to "be all things to all men" definitely applies here, and

About the Author

the Lord keeps adding to that list of things each and every day.

How does she do it all? Experience through every book and teaching the life of an apostle firsthand, and get the insight into how the call of God can make every aspect of your life an incredible adventure.

Read more at www.colette-toach.com

Connect with Colette Toach on Facebook!
www.facebook.com/ColetteToach

Check Colette out on Amazon.com at:
www.amazon.com/author/colettetoach

Recommendations by the Author

Note: All reference of AMI refers to Apostolic Movement International.

If you enjoyed this book, we know you will also love the following books on the prophetic.

Prophetic Essentials

Book 1 of the Prophetic Field Guide Series

By Colette Toach

In this book, you will find out that the call of the prophet goes far deeper than the functions and duties that the prophet fulfills. Anyone flowing in prophetic ministry can carry out tasks similar to the prophet.

If it burns in you to pay any price that is necessary and to stand up and break down the barriers between the Lord Jesus and His Bride, then my friend, you have picked up the right tool that will confirm the fire in your belly and the call of God on your life.

If you go through the pages of this book, you will no longer see prophecy and prophetic ministry as the beginning and end of the prophetic call. You will cross a threshold and be thrust into the fullness of the call and responsibility of God's true prophet.

Colette Toach

PROPHETIC FUNCTIONS

Book 2 of the Prophetic Field Guide Series

By Colette Toach

There is so much more to the prophet than standing up in church and prophesying.

Laid out beautifully so that you can understand and relate, Colette Toach shares from her own personal experiences. She uses both the Word and the Spirit - a rare combination, to drive the point home. Be prepared to live and experience the Lord like never before. This is not fiction... this is your training guide to the prophetic.

PROPHETIC ANOINTING

Book 3 of the Prophetic Field Guide Series

By Colette Toach

God has promised you a visit to the throne room! This is your summons from Almighty God. It is time for you to experience Him face-to-face and heart-to-heart.

Get ready for the meeting of a lifetime. The veils that have hindered the anointing in your life are going to be ripped away, and you are going to shine with His glory in every area of your life.

PROPHETIC BOOT CAMP

Book 4 of the Prophetic Field Guide Series

By Colette Toach

The way of the prophet is one that goes through the cross, surrenders in death and rises up in resurrection power and authority. Deep inside you know that you have not gone through this hard road just to come out defeated. You have paved the way for others.

So, prophet of God, are you ready to sign up for boot camp?

PROPHETIC COUNTER INSURGENCE

Book 6 of the Prophetic Field Guide Series

By Colette Toach

Learn all about the "prophetic super spy", discover strategies that can be used in spiritual warfare, receive stealth training, find the secrets to dealing with fear of the mind, and where spiritual warfare begins and ends.

It is time to become an agent of Christ, capable of striking down the enemy at any time, in any place, and wherever the Lord calls for it. It is time to take the crippling blows of the enemy and turn them into deathly blows of destruction.

PRESENTATION OF PROPHECY

By Colette Toach

You do not need to be a prophet to prophecy and God will not come forcibly on you and make you do anything.

It is indeed a gift of the spirit that can be practiced. By the end of this book, you will be amazed to discover how accessible this gift of the Holy Spirit is to you. You will know the steps 1, 2, 3 of presenting prophecy.

I'M NOT CRAZY - I'M A PROPHET

By Colette Toach

It takes a prophet to know a prophet! You do not have to follow in the footsteps of others before you take the wealth of this book and rise above the pit falls.

That is why only Colette Toach can take the prophetic and dish it out in its truth and cover the subjects included in this book. So are you crazy? Maybe a little, but this book will help you to be the true prophet that God has called you to be!

A.M.I. Prophetic School

www.prophetic-school.com

Whether you are just starting out or have been along the way for some time, we all have questions.

Who better to answer them than another prophet!

With over 18 years of experience, the A.M.I. Prophetic School is the leader in the prophetic realm.

From dedicated lecturers to live streaming and graduation, the A.M.I. Prophetic School is your home away from home.

What Our Prophetic Training Accomplishes

Our extensive training is a full two-year curriculum that will:

1. Identify and confirm your prophetic call
2. Effectively train you to flow in all the gifts of the Spirit
3. Fulfill your purpose as a prophet in the local church
4. Take your hand through the prophetic training process
5. Specialist training in spiritual warfare
6. Arm you for intercession and decree
7. Minister in praise and worship
8. Achieve prophetic maturity

CONTACT INFORMATION

To check out our wide selection of materials, go to:
www.ami-bookshop.com

Do you have any questions about any products?

Contact us at: +1 (760) 466 - 7679
(8am to 5pm California Time, Weekdays Only)

E-mail Address: admin@ami-bookshop.com

Postal Address:

>A.M.I.
>5663 Balboa Ave #416
>San Diego, CA 92111, USA

Facebook Page:
http://www.facebook.com/ApostolicMovementInternational

YouTube Page:
https://www.youtube.com/c/ApostolicMovementInternational

Twitter Page: https://twitter.com/apmoveint

Amazon.com Page: www.amazon.com/author/colettetoach

AMI Bookshop – It's not Just Knowledge, It's **Living Knowledge**

www.ingramcontent.com/pod-product-compliance
Lightning Source LLC
Chambersburg PA
CBHW070635160426
43194CB00009B/1472